TENACITY

SOLVED MURDER

Ronald E Bowers

Former Senior Prosecutor
Los Angeles County District Attorney's Office

Some names and locations have been changed to protect the privacy of individuals connected with this story. Certain events have been inferred from the facts of these cases.

Ronald E. Bowers, Publisher
losangelestruecrime@aol.com

ISBN 978-1-7325281-8-5

First release August 2018
Second release March 2019

TENACITY SOLVED MURDER

INTRODUCTION

The public has been inundated for years with Cop television programs like Dragnet. More recently TV viewers have been bombarded by so many CSI programs. As a result, impressionable people begin to think that crimes are somehow magically solved. Now with all the benefits from forensics, TV viewers believe that there is no need for old-fashioned gumshoe detective work. (The original term *gumshoe* came from shoes made from gum rubber in the late 1800s. Later the word *gumshoe* was used to describe someone sneaking up on someone.)

Over the years writers have created fictional detective characters who have gone about solving crime through their super-sleuth methods. Many years ago in the States most people started their Sunday morning by reading the comics. Everyone was anxious to see how ***Dick Tracy*** was going to catch the bad guys. Tracy was a step ahead of most detectives in that he had a wristwatch he could use as a telephone or radio. This occurred many decades before the cell phone was invented. As a result, comic readers thought Dick Tracy was an amazing detective the way he went about solving crime and catching the bad guys.

The movies introduced the public to detectives who seemed to fall all over themselves in the pursuit of solving their cases. The Pink Panther movies introduce the world to **Inspector Clouseau** who seemed such a buffoon who couldn't do anything right but somehow, he was able to stumble on to the crooks. Television later introduced the public to Peter Falk's character **Sgt. Colombo** who cleverly would outsmart the crook by using Colombo logic. As disheveled as Sgt. Colombo looked, the TV viewer received the impression that appearances were deceiving. It wasn't until Angela Lansbury played the sleuth in ***Murder She Wrote*** that a woman gained fame in figuring out who was the real culprit. This program demonstrated that a woman's intuition shouldn't be discounted when trying to figure out who the real killer was.

The publishing world has produced some rough and tough detectives such as **Mike Hammer** by Mickey Spillane and **Philip Marlowe** by Raymond Chandler. These detectives had character flaws which readers enjoyed hearing about but it was their keen sense of knowing where to look for the crucial evidence that made them seem so smart. However, the two writers who had the greatest impact on the public perception of what real detectives were like would have to be Agatha Christie and Sir Arthur Conan Doyle.

Agatha Christie wrote about her detective character **Hercule Poirot** as he went about narrowing down all the suspects whether it was on the ***Orient Express*** or the Egyptian riverboat in ***Death on the Nile***.

Sir Arthur Conan Doyle created his detective character **Sherlock Holmes** around the turn of the century. Holmes combined the old gumshoe technique with the use of futuristic forensic science. Conan Doyle was on the cutting edge of introducing the public to a new approach in criminology. Even though the character Holmes was fictional, Doyle made him come alive in the minds of the readers. Each one of his 57 separate books introduced the public to new scientific discoveries in criminology.

Doyle used a writing technique that made the exploits of his detective Holmes more appealing to his readers. His stories weren't narrated by Holmes but by Holmes' colleague Dr. Watson. This permitted the reader to feel as though he or she was following behind Holmes walking in Dr. Watson's footsteps. Doyle later admitted that the Dr. Watson character was fictitious but was fashioned after a real-life colleague of Doyle.

What Doyle's Sherlock Holmes book series did was show the public that crimes aren't solved by merely adding more detectives to an investigation. Doyle's character Sherlock Holmes was depicted as an individual who could think outside the box. Conan Doyle was originally educated as a medical doctor and even had a medical practice for several years. With Doyle's medical background he was able to insert in his books medical insight as to items like the cause of death and time of death.

Doyle's unique talent of being a medical doctor and writer allowed him to discuss topics that no other author was capable of writing about. That is why the Sherlock Holmes books were so insightful in showing all the ways a detective needs to approach a crime scene in order to solve the difficult homicide cases. Although Sherlock Holmes is a fictional character, there are dozens of actual detectives in the real world who approach their cases with a Sherlock Holmes mindset.

In my 43 years as a prosecutor with the Los Angeles District Attorney's Office, I have had the opportunity to work with so many supersleuths. It is hard to describe what makes one homicide detective superior to others. I often wondered why certain detectives were better at digging up clues and knowing which ones to pursue and which ones were nothing but red herrings. I found that some detectives seem to have a sixth sense of knowing what tool to pull out of the old criminology toolbox.

I decided to write this **TODAY'S SHERLOCK HOLMES** series to highlight certain detectives who did remarkable jobs in solving problematic cases. I have selected to write about an extraordinary case I personally worked on with one of the most talented detectives. I take you, the reader, through every step of the investigation showing you what worked and what ended up as a waste of time. What I have noticed is that the super detectives have an uncanny ability to spot the obscure clues. You will see that a great detective has to have an abundance of TENACITY. When they end up at a dead end they must have dogged determination to keep on going and shift their focus to other viable clues.

This case we will be examining has perplexed me for years. It involved a residential robbery which ultimately turned into an unfortunate felony murder. The murdered victim's wife has to be one of the bravest women I have ever come across. The crime took place in Woodland Hills, a part of the San Fernando Valley which is considered one of the safest places to live in the City of the Angels.

In 1999, the San Fernando Valley was being inundated with robbers who cruised around looking for potential victims. These robbers were on the lookout for people who appeared to be wealthy. It might be the type of car they were driving such as a Rolls Royce or a person wearing flashy jewelry such as a Rolex or Cartier accessories. The robbers would follow these rich people home and attack them as they pulled into their garages. The robbers seemed to be working in teams of two or three who would rob the wealthy person in their home where they could easily take valuable items from the victims as well as property from their homes.

The suspects made sure that they wouldn't be caught since they robbed the victims in the isolation of victims' houses. Since the robbers wore ski mask and gloves, the victims were unable to provide any useable description of the robbers. They also left no fingerprints or bodily fluids that could be traced back to them. LAPD was feeling the pressure from the media and public to find a way to catch these teams of residential robbers.

This book will focus on one case involving defendant **Boris Graham** and to a lesser extent the codefendant **Kirell Taylor**. The reader will be walking in the footsteps of the lead detective Andrew Powell (Pseudonym) to see how he approached each clue and how he went about examining it. In the closing chapters of the book we will review each of the clues and assess how useful they were in solving this case.

Sir Arthur Conan Doyle's character, Sherlock Holmes, would be proud of how Detective Powell approached this Graham/Taylor case. Although Sherlock Holmes didn't have some of today's forensics tools like DNA, Holmes would have used a similar approach that would have scrutinized each piece of evidence. Sherlock Holmes and Detective Andrew Powell had a lot in common. Both were able to think outside the box and both were willing to take risks. They both understood that most clues lead to dead ends. However, it is their personal persistence and perseverance that allowed them to disregard the endless smokescreen of false clues. They had the wherewithal to concentrate on the clues which would eventually solve what seemed to be an unsolvable case.

One of Sherlock Holmes' famous quotes from his book *The Hound of the Baskervilles* was "There is nothing more stimulating than a case where everything goes against you." This summarizes what Detective Powell may have thought when he first started investigating this Rawlings case. Everything seemed to be going against Detective Powell until the BIG BREAK occurred.

* * *

CONTENTS

Chapter 1 Time to Come Home 1
Chapter 2 Wife Waiting....... 9
Chapter 3 Officers to the Rescue 19
Chapter 4 Bentley Can Be a Fast Car 25
Chapter 5 Violent Crash Site 29
Chapter 6- Running Suspects 35
Chapter 7 Investigating the Crash Site 41
Chapter 8 Checking out the House 47
Chapter 9- Hospital Visit 51
Chapter 10 Need a Description 55
Chapter 11- Getting a Good Description 61
Chapter 12- Investigation 101 65
Chapter 13- *America's Most Wanted* TV Program 69
Chapter 14- Zeroing in on Taylor 75
Chapter 15- Taylor's Trial 83
Chapter 16- Kirell and DNA Expert 87
Chapter 17- Kirell Takes Witness Stand 91
Chapter 18- Kirell Disliked the Detectives....... 95
Chapter 19- Who's the Other Suspect? 99
Chapter 20- Taylor Spilled the Beans 109
Chapter 21- Preparing for Boris' Jury Trial....... 123
Chapter 22- Basic Witnesses for Boris' Trial 131
Chapter 23- Testimony of Detective Powell....... 137
Chapter 24 Kirell Testified....... 139
Chapter 25- Parks Testimony at Boris' Trial....... 143
Chapter 26 Friday Tells the Truth....... 147
Chapter 27- What's DNA Evidence All About? 149
Chapter 28- The English Blooding....... 155
Chapter 29- DNA Database Debate 159
Chapter 30- Using DNA in Boris' Trial....... 163

Chapter 31- Consciousness of Guilt 167
Chapter 32- Time for Argument- Understanding the FACTS 171
Chapter 33- Culpability of the Robbers 181
Chapter 34- Elements of Crimes 185
Chapter 35- Conclusion of Trial 195
Chapter 36- Critique of the Investigation 199
Chapter 37- Epilogue 215
Chapter 38- What Have We Learned? 223
Chapter 39- What We Need to Do 229

CHAPTER 1 TIME TO COME HOME

Monday, February 8, 1999, was like any other day starting a work week. Los Angeles had a light rain just enough to dampen the streets and give the Chamber of Commerce a chance to claim there is no smog in LA. After working all day at his clothing store Christopher Rawlings decided to call it a day. He and his partner operated a high-end men's fashion store called the Gentleman's Quarters in Studio City.

Christopher Rawlings

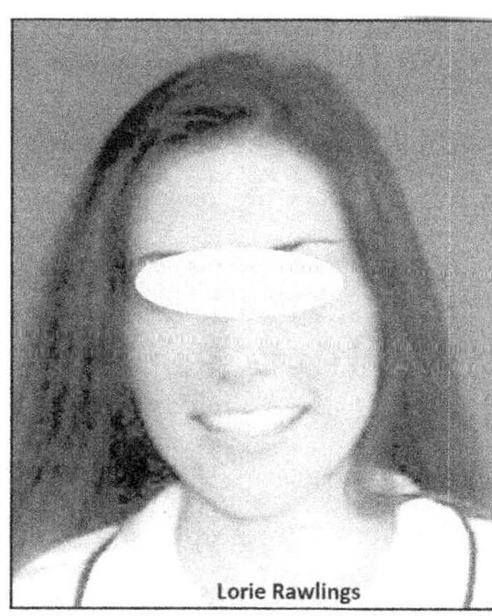

Lorie Rawlings

Christopher had phoned his wife, Lorie (Pseudonym), to find out if she would like him to pick up groceries from the market. She told him what items they needed. He asked about dinner and she indicated that it would be wonderful if he could stop and pick up something for dinner. Christopher enjoyed being physically fit and Lorie took pride in preparing nutritious meals especially at dinner time. When she gave Christopher the option to stop and buy dinner he didn't hesitate. He recognized that this was his chance to get some delicious fast food that he enjoyed instead of a wholesome healthy dinner.

He mentioned that he would stop at a fast food place on Ventura Boulevard. Lorie was busy with the children at home and didn't specify what to buy. Christopher had the perfect opportunity to get what he liked. It didn't take him long to decide and he headed to the Fatburger fast food restaurant to buy some juicy burgers and greasy fries.

Gentleman's Quarters Store

As Christopher walked out of his men's store, he bid farewell to his partner who was straightening things up near the front door. Christopher seemed to have a kick in his step as he walked directly to his white Bentley parked outside the store. Christopher wasn't shy in telling the world that he was a person on his way to the top. Christopher could be described as a showy guy who wanted to be recognized as a man of means.

The white Bentley was parked in the first stall just across from the entrance to his fashionable store. Christopher's mindset was that his classy Bentley sent a message to potential customers that this was the place where the rich and famous shop. He pushed the button on his key ring and his Bentley lit up. Since there had been a light drizzle, his Bentley glistened with all its lights flashing on.

Christopher looked at his watch to see what time it was. Of course, his watch was none other than a Rolex from the Presidential series. As he got into his Bentley he immediately sat down in the driver's seat as a confident smile came over his face. He wasn't trying to show off to others however, he was a person who thoroughly enjoyed his level of success from all his hard work.

He eased his way out of the parking lot onto busy Ventura Boulevard and headed first to the local Ralph's Market. His next challenge was finding a place to park in the market's congested parking lot. Needless to say, it was the busiest time to shop and it seemed that there were no empty spaces. Christopher considered his Bentley like a precious member of the family. He didn't want anyone to ding his cherished Bentley when people swung open their car doors. He circled around to the back-parking row and found an empty space and parked.

By then the weather had turned from a mist to a heavy drizzle causing Christopher to look for an umbrella. Not seeing one in the backseat, he decided to brave the elements by running between the drops. Since he was well familiar with the layout of the market, it didn't take him long to find everything that his wife needed. He gazed at all the checkout lines to see which would be the fastest. He maneuvered his shopping cart to the shortest line. He then noticed that one of the customers in front of him had a shopping cart which was stuffed full of groceries. At that point Christopher realized he had selected the wrong line but it was too late to move since the other lines had gotten longer.

He smiled to himself that he was going to have to wait even though he didn't like the idea. His eyes started staring at the tabloid rack which included National Enquirer and others with their teasing and tantalizing headlines. One article fascinated him enough for him to pick up the rag and flip through the pages. Unfortunately, he got to the cashier before he could find the article he was looking for. Within minutes he was checked out and pushing his shopping cart to the back row where he had parked. He placed all the groceries in the trunk since he didn't want to take a chance of anything spilling inside the interior of his magnificent Bentley.

Then it was off to the Fatburger just down the street. He placed his order and the only major decision he had to make was whether to supersize his order. He knew that his wife would make some snide comment if he brought home a supersized food order. He demonstrated some restraint and said, "no." Within minutes he had his completed order and his next major decision was where to place all the bags of food so they wouldn't spill in the plush interior of his Bentley.

After he secured everything in place, he headed home. By then Christopher's mind was on automatic-pilot mode and he was settling into a satisfying mood. His nose got a whiff of the fragrant fries and he couldn't wait to get home to consume them. He turned up the music on his car radio. He enjoyed listening to the Bentley's highly sophisticated sound system. Faith Hill's huge hit of 1999, ***There You Be*** was being played on the radio. The lyrics were firmly etched into Christopher's memory as he mouthed the words from the song. The song was about two lovers who become parted in their wonderful life. Little did Christopher know how poetic these lyrics would become within the next few minutes of his life.

When I think back on these times,
And the dreams we left behind,
I'll be glad' cause I was blessed to get,
To have you in my life.

When I think back on these days,
I look and see your face,
You were right there for me.

In my dreams I'll always see you soar above the sky
In my heart there'll always be a place for you,
For all my life,
I'll keep a part of you with me,
And everywhere I am there you'll be.

Christopher had the world at his feet. The day before, he had celebrated his 30th birthday. He was born in Davenport, Iowa in 1969 and after preschool his family moved to Southern California. They lived in the Calabasas area where he went to Viewpoint School for his elementary years. Later he went to Crespi High School in Encino where he excelled in sports especially football. Although he was only 5' 8" he had dogged determination which made him a star player. He did well in track and wrestling based on his competitive nature that helped him to succeed.

He graduated in 1987 from high school and wasn't certain what he wanted to do with his life. He had a burning desire to make money and started following the college route by enrolling in San Diego State University. After a year he returned home to attend Valley College for another year. Then he headed North to go to UC at Berkeley but that didn't seem to capture his imagination. The next thing his family knew was that he had joined the US Marine Corps and was going through boot camp.

Christopher liked the competitiveness and enjoyed pushing himself to be the best. He served in Japan and when his time was up he returned to the Valley doing computer work. He bounced from several jobs always looking for a company where he could make a whole heap of money.

In 1994, he met Lorie at a restaurant in Calabasas. He was a handsome dude and was the type of man every mother would want their daughter to meet and eventually marry. Within a short period of time they were married and started a family. They had two daughters and Christopher became the perfect family man.

Lorie came from a middle-class family from Granada Hills in the Valley. She only wanted the simple life for her family. However, Christopher had a flair for the nice things in life especially cars. He loved fancy cars and enjoyed driving around the Valley in expensive sports cars. Lorie would ask Christopher whether they could afford such luxuries and he assured her that his various businesses and investments were paying off. Christopher's source of income was always a mystery to Lorie. All she knew was that he was always able to make ends meet. He told his wife that she was in charge of the house and their daughters and it was his job to provide for them.

On that drizzly Monday evening Christopher pulled into his driveway. He couldn't help but think what a lucky guy he was. He had a beautiful home in an upscale area of the San Fernando Valley with a wonderful wife, Lorie. To fully round out the perfect family he had two healthy cute children he adored. He reached up on his car's sun visor and pushed the button on the remote-controlled garage opener. Instantaneously the garage door magically started opening. Every time he used it he thought to himself how wonderful life would be if everything would respond to a push of a button.

Front of Rawlings House

The interior garage light came on and he slowly drove the car inside and automatically put the car in 'PARK.' He left the ignition on so he could hear the end of Faith Hill's song. He then pushed the garage-door button and he could hear the whiny door close behind him. He stepped out of the driver's door as he spun back inside the car to retrieve the fast food. As he was turning, he heard a loud male voice yell something at him. That was when he pivoted around and saw a horrific sight.

CHAPTER 2 WIFE WAITING

Some might label Lorie Rawlings as a trophy wife since she was attractive and always appeared well groomed and fashionably dressed. She was more than a pretty Valley Girl. She adored her loving husband. She was now 26 years old and pleased to have married an attractive chap who seemed to make things happen. As a result, they lived well in a stylish house in Woodland Hills. It was bigger and fancier than any house Lorie had ever dreamed of. It was spacious with five bedrooms which was plenty of room for their family of four. The backyard was ideal for entertaining with its tempting swimming pool and room for children's toys.

The birth of their two children seemed to round out Lorie's life. She truly had to believe that she was living the great Camelot life in suburbia. Lorie had her very own Suburban parked in the driveway. Lorie recognized how fortunate they were as a family and took pride in what they had built for themselves. To some housekeeping was a chore but Lorie took pride in seeing that her house was spotless with everything in its appropriate place.

On this particular Monday evening she had her hands full with an active five-year-old and an infant still in the crib upstairs. Even though she had asked her husband to pick up food she still had to set the table for dinner. After talking to Christopher on the phone, she went back to the kitchen to clean up everything on the sink board and placed all the dried dishes back in the cupboards. Since she was hungry, she was eagerly awaiting her husband arriving with the food for dinner.

Lorie could hear the garage door opener make a whining sound as the garage door slowly crept upward. Her ears pricked up as she heard the Bentley pull into the two-car garage with the radio blaring. Many times she had told Christopher to tone

down the music but he loved the great sounds from the Bentley's sound system. His feeling was that when he was driving alone what harm was the loud music to anyone else. Lorie didn't argue with him since that was one of those annoying traits she could overlook.

Lorie concentrated on finishing the setting of the table and lost track of what Christopher was doing. After a minute or so the music was still blaring and she could hear other sounds coming from the garage. At first it seemed like yelling and it didn't make any sense since Christopher was supposedly all by himself. Lorie shook her head slightly wondering what was delaying her husband. Now the other sounds were causing Lorie some concern. She had just picked up some silverware from inside the dishwasher and she decided to step over to the door to the garage to see what was delaying Christopher.

She walked over to the laundry room which had a door that entered into the garage. She slowly opened the door which gave her a view into the garage. To her shock she saw her husband on his knees with two men standing over him dressed in black with ski masks on. Both men were pointing guns at Christopher's head.

Looking into Garage from Laundry Room

Laundry Room

Lorie couldn't believe her eyes. She froze in place not knowing what to do. She could see that the men were concentrating on Christopher on the floor and not looking in her direction. Lorie moved backward without creating any noise. She slowly closed the laundry door without making a sound. She turned around rapidly and walked back on her tiptoes so not to make any noise. As she returned to the kitchen her mind was spinning around not knowing what to do next.

She reacted by going over to the portable phone in the kitchen and grabbed it so she could call 9-1-1. She could hear the voices in the garage grow louder. She recognized Christopher's voice as he was shrieking out at the masked men. Lorie's eyes looked over to her five-year-old who was quietly playing with her toys on a kid's table. Fear came over her wondering how to keep the children safe. As a mother what should she do?

Since she had never been a victim of a crime she didn't know how to react. Her sense of fear was turning to panic. She felt all alone in making a life and death decision. She gazed at her innocent child who was totally oblivious to the danger that was about to beset them. She stepped over to where her daughter was playing and tried to grab her by the shoulders. However, since Lorie's hands were full with the cordless phone in one hand and a hand full of silverware in the other, she could only nudge her daughter forward toward the front door. When she reached the entry area she was confronted with one of the most perilous dilemmas that any mother could face.

There was the front door that she and her older daughter could run out to safety escaping the masked men in the garage. Just as she was about to reach the front door knob she froze in her tracks. Her mind filled with the sight of her precious baby who was asleep in her crib upstairs. Next to her were the stairs leading upstairs to the infant's room. As a mother she couldn't leave behind her defenseless baby. She pulled her oldest child over toward the stairs and directed her to climb up the stairs. Her daughter couldn't quite understand what was going on so Lorie in a calm quiet voice told her to go up to the baby's room.

As they reached the top of the stairs, she could still hear the shouting coming from the garage but the voices were too muffled to be able to make out what was being said. As she kept prodding her daughter to quickly move toward the infant's room, she knew that within moments she could scoop up her infant daughter and then escape. She darted into the master bedroom in hopes that there was someone there to save her and her children. She stood helplessly at the end of the master bed and wondered what advice Christopher would give her in such a desperate situation.

She looked at her hands one holding the cordless phone and the other holding several spoons, a fork and a table knife. All of a sudden, her brain gave a command to her hand to drop the useless silverware which fell on top the plush bedroom carpet. As she stood there paralyzed with fear her eyes fixated on her jewelry box on the dresser filled with her favorite fine jewelry.

She loved her husband for many reasons but one of Christopher's positive traits that Lorie loved was the fact that he would surprise her with gifts of exquisite jewelry. Lorie had a soft spot for Cartier jewelry especially the Jaguar collection. She had received bracelets and earrings that cost thousands of dollars which she obsessed over. Christopher's generosity was appreciated by Lorie as a symbol as to how deep their love was for each other.

Should she take the time to retrieve her fine jewelry which she greatly treasured? At that moment she could hear what sounded like the laundry room door slam against the washing machine. The loud noise jolted Lorie to refocus on how she was going to protect her children.

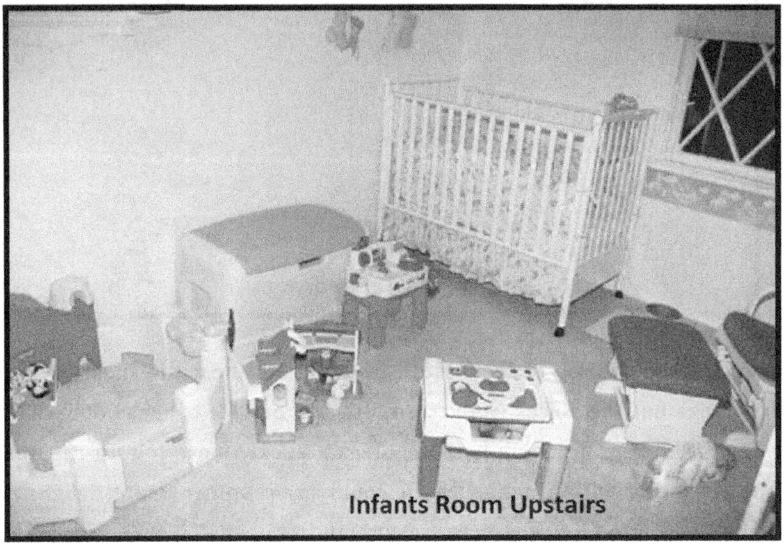

Infants Room Upstairs

She turned and clutched her oldest one by the clothing and practically dragged her into the infant's room. She could hear the attackers walking around downstairs. She moved into the infant's room and saw her darling baby daughter in the crib. Running over to the crib she picked up her infant and stood there motionless. Now she realized that her plan of escape out the front door was no longer possible.

Her older daughter was frightened not knowing what to do so she wrapped her arms around her mother's leg. Now Lorie had no place to run to and her eyes stared directly at the window of the baby's room. As the noise from downstairs grew louder Lorie felt that her back was against the wall and no place to go to. There was no closet to hide in or large furniture to hide behind.

Lorie throughout her life had been a fighter and some would say she was a 'go-getter.' Growing up she was one of those independent thinkers who had learned early in life that women were capable of doing anything. Her eyes fixated on the small window of the infant's room. As scared as Lorie was, she remembered when they bought the house the sales broker had shown her and her husband a ledge on the roof that ran the length of the upstairs windows. They always wondered why the builder of the house had built that ledge outside the windows.

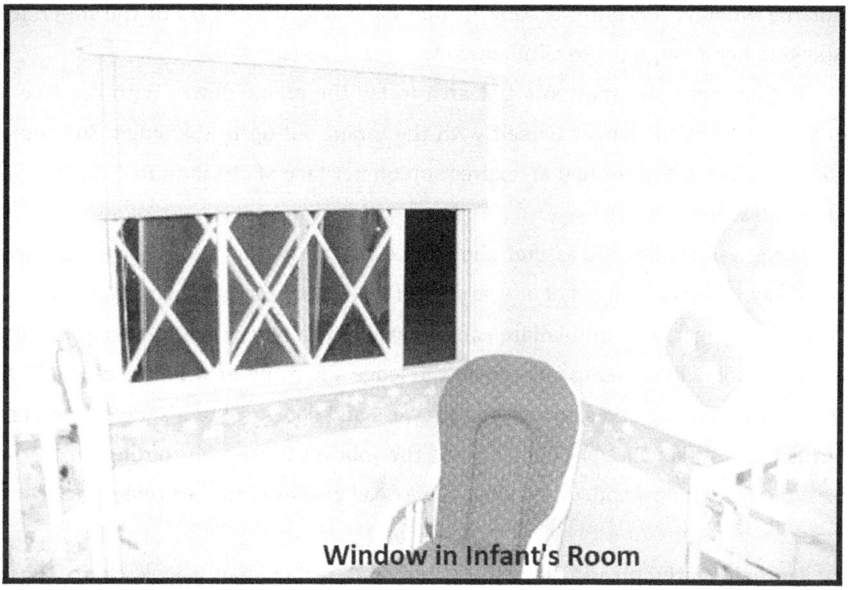

Window in Infant's Room

Lorie placed the baby back in the crib and walked over to the window and quietly slid it open. Immediately she was blocked by a window screen that prevented her from getting out on the ledge. It didn't take a nanosecond before Lorie had pushed open the screen. She stuck her head out of the open window and looked at the ledge. Was this a good idea to take an infant and her five-year-old daughter out onto this narrow ledge? She could see that if they slipped off the ledge, they would slide down the slippery roof and land on the hard concrete driveway.

Her mind was assessing the situation and her maternal instincts were telling her that it was too risky. As Lorie pulled her head back into the room, she could hear voices coming up the stairs approaching the master bedroom. Realizing she had only moments before becoming a victim of a home invasion robbery, she pulled a chair over to the open window. She pulled her clinging older daughter off her leg and lifted her onto the ledge outside. She realized that she didn't have time to instruct her daughter on the safety aspect of walking on a narrow ledge on the roof.

As soon as she had her daughter outside on the roof, she quickly turned her attention on her infant daughter in the crib. With one arm she firmly grasped the infant and leaned over to pick up the cordless phone she had placed on the dresser. She took one step toward the chair and placed one foot on it raising her up to lean out the window. Carrying a baby in one hand and the phone in the other wasn't allowing her enough lift to climb outside.

At that point she spotted a flat area to lay the phone down. With her free hand she was able to maneuver herself with the infant out on to the ledge. She could see that her older daughter had an expression on her face of absolute fear that no parent wants to see.

Lorie was on her knees and she turned her head and looked down toward the driveway. She thought what a scary sight and immediately turned her head away from the danger. Her immediate concern was the safety of her children on this wet slippery ledge. Even being outside on the ledge she could hear loud male voices with occasional opening and slamming of drawers and doors. All of a sudden, her concern turned to the fact that she didn't want the robbers to find her hiding on the ledge. Leaving the window wide open would be a dead giveaway to the crooks.

Lorie gingerly turned herself around and inched her way back to the open window. As Lorie move back to the window, she decided to pull the window blinds down thereby totally concealing the fact that the window was missing a window screen. With her one hand bracing her she reached inside and pulled the blind cord down. As she removed her hand, she quietly slid the window closed.

Throughout this entire ordeal Lorie was frantically trying to dial 9-1-1 for help. Now being safely on the ledge, she concentrated on her attempts to alert the police what was going on. She had related to the police dispatcher her address explaining that two men in black were pointing guns at her husband. Being out on the ledge Lorie could now talk louder and clearer to the dispatcher.

She explained that she could still hear the men ransacking her house. After several minutes the noise coming from the house subsided. Then she thought she heard her husband scream for 'dear life.' Seconds later the garage door made the sound that it was opening. She was able to relate to the dispatcher that the Bentley was slowly backing out of the driveway. She couldn't see who was in the Bentley as it rolled across the street hitting the curb on the other side of the roadway. She knew that Christopher wasn't driving since he wouldn't allow his Bentley to bump into the curb.

As Lorie was talking to the dispatcher, she could see two police units on her street. Thank God the ordeal was almost over and the police had come to their rescue. Lorie grabbed both children and hugged them tightly not wanting to let go of them.

CHAPTER 3 OFFICERS TO THE RESCUE

Two LAPD officers were working together in a police car that drizzling Monday evening. They had had their dinner break and were patrolling the Woodland Hills area. This was a laid-back assignment for any officers since there was so little that happened at the far West end of the San Fernando Valley. Because it was an affluent residential area there were few calls for police services. The two officers heard the broadcast of a 'hot prowl burglary' on Quedo Drive. They were slightly disappointed since they weren't assigned the call.

Their regret was short-lived when the dispatcher assigned them to back up the original unit on this burglary call. Such a hot call would spice up their uneventful day which had consisted of humdrum shoplifting by juveniles. All those uneventful calls involved nothing more than reading the riot act to the kids. Since the store owners didn't want to waste their time having to appear in court to testify, the officers ended up letting the kids go.

These officers were familiar with Quedo Drive so they took several side streets to reach the specific address. In the process they got to the Rawlings residence first. Seeing that the assigned unit hadn't arrived they pulled to the curb and stopped just West of the house. Since the call had come out as a 'hot prowl burglary' they both exited their vehicle with flashlights in hand expecting they might have to look around in a dark backyard to apprehend the burglar.

The two of them rushed up to the side of the property and tried to find cover in the shrubbery next to the garage. They could see that the garage door was closed but there was a crack of light shining from under the garage door. As they stood just outside of the garage they could vaguely hear several male voices. "You've gonna stay down! We're gonna keep you down." The officers didn't know what to read into such statements. Next they distinctly heard two car doors slam.

To their surprise they heard the garage door start rolling up. They immediately darted back behind an elm tree on the side corner of the garage. From their concealed position they could barely see a large white vehicle inching out of the garage and onto the driveway. As it came into full view of the officers it appeared to be a Rolls Royce. Both officers looked at each other with wonderment since they had never seen such an expensive car on a typical burglary call.

What were they to read into the fact that a Rolls Royce appeared to be coasting down the slightly sloped driveway? It seemed like they were watching a slow-motion replay on TV as the car coasted across the street striking the curb on the other side. Were the occupants of the car suspects or victims? The other possibility was that the officers had responded to the wrong house.

The officers seemed frozen with disbelief. Both officers were holding a flashlight in one hand and the other hand holding a walkie-talkie radio. By this time the officers got a frontal view of the car and they could see the radiator grill of the vehicle was that of a Bentley not a Rolls Royce. Although many people wouldn't recognize the difference, the officers wanted to put out a broadcast about the vehicle leaving and they wanted to be accurate as to their description.

As the officers stepped out from behind the tree they could see another LAPD unit approaching the house. Since the responding officers weren't able to quickly return to their unit, they used their walkie talkie to broadcast the description and direction of the Bentley. The officers could see their partners take up the pursuit of the Bentley.

The remaining officers decided to check out the house. They were constantly talking to the dispatcher who was relating that the resident, Lorie, was telling them that her husband should be somewhere in the house. She kept explaining that she had seen at least two men wearing masks both in possession of guns. The officers realized that they needed to clear the house to make sure the masked men were no longer present.

Since the garage door was wide open and the lights were on, the officers approached the laundry room door which opened into the kitchen. By this time the adrenaline rush was hitting the officers. They wanted to free Lorie and locate her husband but they were concerned about the whereabouts of the two masked men with guns.

The officers methodically did what they have been taught as to how to enter closed doors when someone may be armed inside. This is a slow process but is necessary so none of the officers end up being shot. Eventually the officers work their way upstairs and by that time they were met by Lorie in the infant's room. She was in the process of retrieving her children from the ledge on the roof.

Rawlings House

She was greatly relieved that the nightmare was over. Now she knew that her two children were safe. Except for a few scratches she had survived the ordeal. Her heart was pounding so hard she had difficulty catching her breath. She rapidly explained what had happened. Then she asked to see her husband, Christopher. The officers didn't know how to respond since they hadn't found anyone else in the house. Since both Lorie and the officers had seen the Bentley back out of the garage, they had to wonder whether he had been in the car.

After more checking of the yard and closets Christopher was nowhere to be found. At that point the officers notified the dispatcher that a victim may be in the Bentley that they were pursuing. The officers asked Lorie if she would take a look around to determine if anything was missing. With her oldest child clinging to her leg and her baby in her arms she slowly moved into the master bedroom at the end of the hallway.

Jewelry Box on Dresser

As she stepped in, her eyes went directly to her jewelry box on top of the dresser near the bed. Under her breath she muttered "Oh my God." She could see the jewelry drawers had been pulled out and some were lying empty on the top of the dresser. Another one was on the floor. As she looked at the empty drawers of missing jewelry, she felt that she and her home had been violated. How could another person come into their house and take things that were precious to her? At that moment her baby in her arms cried softly and immediately Lorie snapped back into reality. Her motherly eyes turned away from the missing jewelry and focused on the little baby's face.

Lorie was learning one true fact of life. Mere possessions can be replaced. Yet the well-being of one's family is irreplaceable. She squeezed her baby tight and took her other hand and lovingly pulled her eldest child closer to her leg. Lorie reassessed what was of value to her and wanted to thank God that her precious children had survived this ordeal. As soon as Christopher comes home, Lorie would once again be surrounded by everything she truly loved and adored.

CHAPTER 4 BENTLEY CAN BE A FAST CAR

Two other officers were responding to the 'hot prowl' call on Quedo Drive and the only car they saw in the area that passed them was a white Bentley. They heard over the police radio that the suspects were leaving in a white Bentley. They turned their police unit around to follow the Bentley that was proceeding up Kelvin Avenue. The officers were a little apprehensive to go into a pursuit of a Bentley. They didn't want to be caught in the situation of stopping a prominent citizen in the community who had a 'lead foot.'

People who drove Bentleys were often part of the rich and famous class. The call didn't come out as a stolen Bentley but the original call was regarding a 'hot prowl' and their colleagues only saying "Suspects leaving in a Bentley." Neither officer had ever heard of a burglar driving a Bentley.

As they turned their police car to follow the Bentley, they hoped to receive further information. But there wasn't anything further broadcasted regarding the Bentley. It didn't take long before the officers realized that the Bentley was pulling away from their pathetic old 'Ford Crown Vic' police car. The officers wanted some assurance that whoever was driving the Bentley was a lawbreaker of some type.

Kelvin Avenue was never intended as a race track especially on a rainy night. The officers were thankful that it was late in the evening and no one was out on the streets. As they went into pursuit mode, they notified other police units where they were headed. The idea was to get police units ahead of the pursuit. However, it isn't easy to know which way a suspect's vehicle is headed. The officers realized that they were approaching Ventura Boulevard but it was unknown whether the Bentley would turn left or right.

As the officers drove north on Kelvin Avenue, they were hitting speeds of close to 100 mph. Then they saw the Bentley make an abrupt right turn on Ventura Boulevard. The Bentley skidded to the side almost striking several cars on the other side of the wide street.

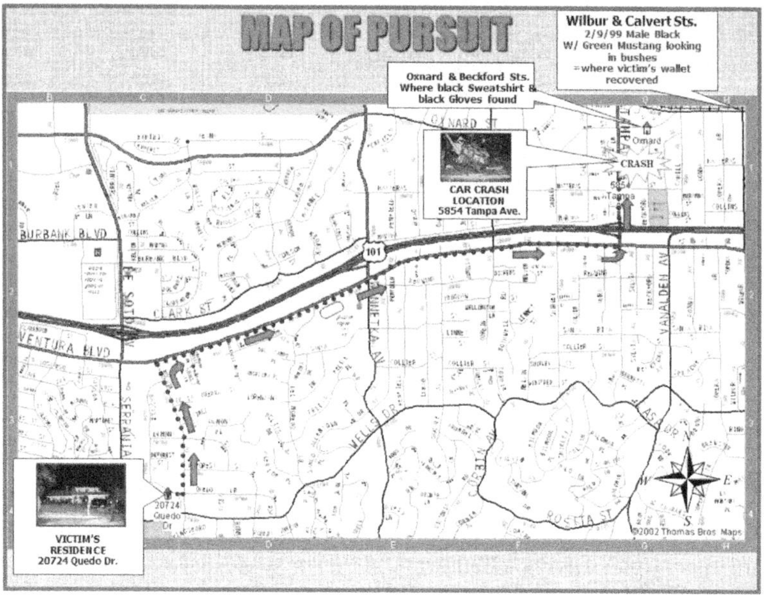

The officers recognized that they needed to reduce their speed if they didn't want to end up causing a traffic accident. Although their old Ford Crown Vic had heavy duty suspension, they knew they were no match for the Bentley. They broadcasted that the Bentley was then headed eastbound on Ventura Boulevard in hopes that other units could get in position to help with the pursuit.

They had their siren blaring and all the emergency lights on as they raced eastbound on Ventura Boulevard. Having to slow down to make the right turn on Ventura had cost the officers precious time. Now the Bentley was so far ahead that it appeared as a mere speck in the distance. The driving officer pressed the accelerator to the metal and the Crown Vic tried to pick up speed but as they came to each intersection they had to slow down in order not to strike other traffic.

The pursuing officers recognized that catching the Bentley wasn't realistic. Their only hope was that another police unit would take up the chase down the line. A police unit responded on Ventura Boulevard near Tampa Avenue. The unit waited and the officers could see the Bentley speeding east on Ventura Boulevard. As the Bentley reached the intersection of Tampa Avenue the car made a wide arc of a turn proceeding northbound on Tampa.

The officers estimated that the Bentley was traveling 80 mph when it made the turn. The tires squealed but the Bentley remained upright and didn't tip over. This new police unit repositioned itself to follow the Bentley. The driver of the Bentley seemed intent on escaping. He continued to maneuver around cars that were in front of him.

It was hard to know why the Bentley was starting to fishtail. Was the driver not familiar with driving a Bentley or was the wet roads causing the erratic driving? As they headed up Tampa there was traffic in all the lanes. The Bentley driver maneuvered over to the right lane in order to squeeze through a pack of cars. A small Chevrolet Cavalier was occupying the slow lane of traffic. The Bentley abruptly came up from behind and accidentally nicked the rear of the little Chevrolet.

Since the Bentley hit it with such force the small Cavalier spun around causing the Bentley to totally push in the rear side of the little car. In the process the Cavalier spun around in circles as it struck everything on the right side of the street including a light standard and mailboxes. However, the Bentley careened off of the Cavalier and headed for a tall high-voltage power pole which it sheared off at the base. This impact caused the Bentley to swivel sideways into another light standard and eventually coming to rest against a large tree in the middle of someone's front yard. The force of the crash caused the trunk of the Bentley of fly open and some items came flying out of the trunk.

Chevrolet Hit by Bentley

CHAPTER 5 VIOLENT CRASH SITE

As the pursuing police unit arrived at the crash site the question was what to do? What concerned them was the fact that they noticed that the high voltage lines were arcing on the ground. One of the wires flipped over and landed on the Bentley causing a large flash. Within seconds flames spread all over the engine compartment engulfing the front end of the car. Since the crash had knocked down the power pole, all the neighborhood lights and street lights flickered several times and then everything went dark.

The officers were faced with a blackout situation with electrified high power lines throwing sparks on anything they touched. Since it had just rained the officers knew if they touched the Bentley they could be electrocuted. At this initial stage they needed to contain the crash site to prevent anyone from being shocked. They informed the dispatcher to contact the Los Angeles City Water and Power Department to have a crew respond to cut off the power.

Bentley against Power Pole

Under the existing situation the police felt helpless in trying to render aid to anyone injured in the accident. All they could do was to maintain a safe distance from the Bentley. Because of all the flames from the fire of the Bentley the officers were able to see a least one person crawl out of the interior of the Bentley. The person was dressed all in black making it impossible to see where the person went. Within moments the person blended into the blacked-out neighborhood.

Minutes later the fire trucks arrived and they carefully sprayed water on the Bentley making sure that they didn't get shocked by the live wires. Eventually the utility crews were successful in turning the power off and began to assess what needed to be done to restore power. Then the officers gingerly entered the area next to the Bentley. Even though the DWP supervisor said that the power was off, the officers went out of their way to avoid touching any of the many wires still dangling on the tree and those lying on the ground.

Several of the officers with flashlights in their hands cautiously walked around the rear of the Bentley to approach the area of the driver's open door. The Bentley was resting on part of the power pole causing the car to come to rest on a strange angle. As they got nearer, they shined their lights into the interior of the Bentley to see if there were any occupants remaining in the car. All they could see were large white air bags which had deployed and were still pushing against the car seat. The officers were satisfied that there were no passengers in the car who might need attention.

Bentley on Light Pole

Slowly the officers stepped over several branches to get to the trunk of the Bentley. To their surprise the trunk was wide open. As they shined their flashlights in the trunk, they could see that it was empty except for several grocery items.

Bentley Trunk Flew Open

The officers radioed that the Bentley was clear with no victims. Someone directed the officers' attention to what looked like a body some 45 feet northeast of the Bentley. Both officers focused their flashlights in the direction of the body.

Cautiously they walked closer to the body and could see that it appeared to be a male dressed in casual clothes. This person wasn't moving but they could hear a slight moaning. One officer got on his radio to report the finding of a victim of the accident. As they got closer, they shined the light on the victim's face and observed blood covering his entire head. What was peculiar was that the male didn't appear to have any other injuries besides the head.

Where Christopher was Found

Since the Bentley was still smoldering, the two officers grabbed the victim by the arms and began pulling him away from the car fire. The officers looked at each other wondering if they would be yelled at by the paramedics for moving the victim. Or if the victim was dead, the homicide detectives would be yelling at them for disturbing the homicide crime scene. As the officers got to a certain point, they both decided that they had gone far enough and gently dropped the victim's arms. It wasn't worth getting into trouble and having to write up reports justifying their actions for moving a body.

By that time there were numerous black and white units surrounding the area. The officers decided to remain with this male victim until the paramedics arrived. They had heard that the original broadcast was a 'hot prowl' with a pursuit. Was this injured male one of the suspects or possibly a victim? Should they handcuff this individual and treat him as a suspect? The officers were relieved as the paramedics arrived and took over the care of this injured male.

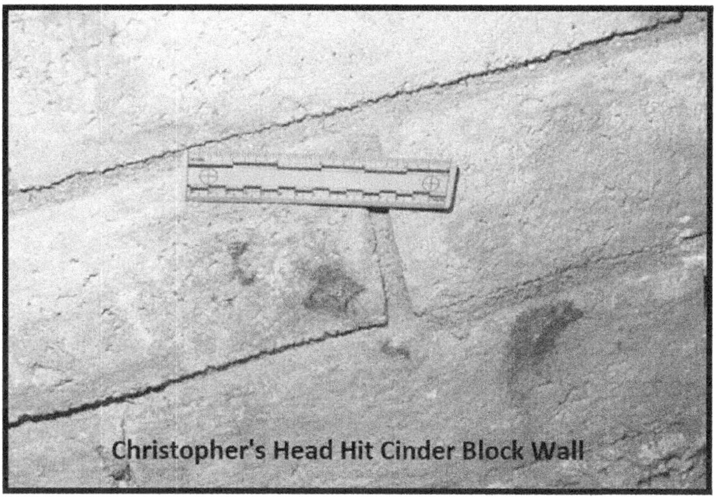

Christopher's Head Hit Cinder Block Wall

The paramedics examined the man's head and said something to each other while shaking their heads. The officers stood back not knowing the severity of the head injury. The paramedics indicated that the person had such severe head trauma that he shouldn't be moved. The paramedics used a splint to stabilize the person's head. Very gently they lifted him onto a gurney and said to the officers that they needed to immediately transport the individual to Northridge Hospital.

The paramedics were in such a hurry they didn't ask any questions about whether the person had been moved. The officers stood there looking at each other and a faint grin came over their face recognizing they had just dodged a bullet. Even though the officers thought they were saving the person's life by moving him away from the fire, no doubt the paramedics wouldn't see it that way. Any movement of such seriously injured individual could be fatal.

CHAPTER 6- RUNNING SUSPECTS

While the officers were concerned with the injured party, they could hear their radio informing all the officers in the area to try to track down the suspects who had been seen running through yards near the crash site.

Dani Yacovone (Pseudonym) was driving his car near Tampa Avenue when he saw this Bentley roar past him at a high rate of speed. A short distance behind that Bentley, there were two police cars with red lights and siren in pursuit of it. Out of curiosity this witness turned north on Tampa to follow the pursuit. Almost immediately this witness had a second thought as how smart it was to follow the speeding vehicles. All of a sudden this driver saw the Bentley collide with a small blue Chevrolet Cavalier.

The impact of these two cars caused both cars to go spinning. The tiny Chevrolet came to rest against a light standard. The Bentley continued flying sideways for another 300 feet and eventually sheared off a power pole and came to rest under a huge tree. This accident caused debris to go flying in all directions. He could see both police cars come to an abrupt halt as the power lines were arcing all over the ground.

This driver, Mr. Yacovone slowly preceded behind the police cars and stopped a safe distance from the mangled Bentley. He could see flames coming from the engine compartment and seeming to be spreading toward the cab of the car. The driver had an unobstructed view of the driver's side door which had ended up wide open. Since the accident had happened only seconds earlier, he was concerned with the safety of the occupants of the Bentley.

Then he saw a person climb out through the open driver's door and run away from the police cars and disappeared into the darkness on the east side of Tampa Avenue. Later he gave a description of the driver as a male black, 5' 8" to 6' tall, medium build, 20 to 26 years of age wearing a ski mask, burgundy jacket, and dark pants CLUE#1.

Seconds later he saw what he believed to be the passenger crawl out of driver's door; he appeared to be limping slightly. This witness's description of this suspect was male black 5'7" to 5' 11"tall, medium build and wearing dark pants. This witness couldn't see in what direction he ran. One of the officers on the scene wrote down the suspects' descriptions and conveyed the information to the dispatcher.

As the suspects escaped into the neighborhood they were seen by residents. David Jack (pseudonym) had just stepped out of his house when he heard a loud crash and within seconds the power to his house went out. He didn't know what to think as to what had happened when he heard some noise on the side of his house. He took a few steps to the side and saw a black male come running toward him. The man came within 15 feet of him. Both men had a surprised look on their faces.

Mr. Jack was caught off guard and didn't know what to say. He uttered, "What's happening?" The man turned his face toward him and responded, "There's a lot of shit going on over there." Mr. Jack didn't know how to react to that information and just stood there. The man just turned toward the gate on the side of the house and continued running. Later Mr. Jack gave the police a description of that man being a male black wearing dark clothing.

Another neighbor, the Lozanos (Pseudonym), had a similar encounter; however they were inside their house when they heard someone on the side of their house. They went to their side window and slightly pulled up the blinds. Both the husband and wife saw a male black walk through their backyard and jump over a cinder block wall. Afterward they walked over to the wall and noticed shoe prints in the mud. They contacted LAPD and provided them with the information. The next day someone from the CSI crew came out and photographed the shoe prints and made plaster casts of the prints. CLUE # 2

More residents of the neighborhood called LAPD 9-1-1 operator. Mr. Sorentino was surprised when the power went out. Initially he thought it was caused by the rainstorm that passed through earlier in the evening. Then to his surprise he saw a male black jump a fence and start running past the front of his house. He told the operator that this person was between 25 to 30 years of age wearing a long-sleeve gray or white shirt with some sort of emblem on the front.

Mr. Sorentino wasn't the type of citizen who refused to get involved. He always complained when others in the community didn't help out in fighting crime. While talking to the operator he went outside and got into his car and started following the suspect who was running down the street. He was able to give the operator a step by step description of exactly where the suspect was located. The suspect may have realized he was being followed and crossed over the railroad tracks and jumped a chain link fence and disappeared from view.

Other residents got involved including John Short (Pseudonym) who stepped out on his back porch with his flashlight after the power went out to see how large an area was affected. He heard a slight sound and shined his light on the roof of his garage. At first he couldn't believe his eyes. There stood a male black or possibly Hispanic looking directly down at him. Although the person was only about 15 feet away, he didn't get a thorough look at him. The person quickly turned and jumped down and disappeared.

As time went on an Oren Aaron (Pseudonym) and a friend were seated in his car parked on Calvert Street near Tampa Avenue. It was like an out-of-mind experience when they both saw a person come out of nowhere. They described him as a black male 5' 9" tall, between 165 to 185 pounds, clean shaven, very short hair, and wearing a white T-white with some type of college logo on it.

What frightened them to death was the fact that this person ran up to their car and started banging on the hood with his bare hands. They felt trapped in this car. What should they do? They didn't know whether the person was injured and needed help. But what happened next really scared them. This man tried to talk but seemed to be too much out of breath. The most they could understand him to say was, "I'll give you $1,000 if you will drive me out of this area." The two men in the car looked at each other and shook their head as they pulled away trying not to strike him. Immediately the passenger used his cell phone to call 9-1-1 and explained what had happened to them.

Mary Vargas (Pseudonym) was driving her older Mazda on Erwin Street several streets from the crash site. She had her school books spread out over the passenger seat with her purse. As she approached a red signal she stopped. Out of nowhere came a male black who started pounding on the hood of her car. Years ago, as a young woman, she always had the fear of something like this happening. In her mind she had figured out how she would handle it.

However, when it really happened to her she was so frightened that she froze in place. This black man moved from the front of the car to her driver's door and pulled on the door handle. Her attention was directed to using both her hands to keep the door closed. Her car was stopped at the intersection and she couldn't leave. Undoubtedly the man's adrenaline was flowing and he soon became so muscular that he was able to pry open the door.

She had read newspaper articles how young women were raped in their cars. She was always critical of those women for not fighting back. As the man reached in he grabbed her with both hands and with one forceful pull had her out of the car. All she could think to do was to try to resist. As a result the man struck her in the face several times. She couldn't tell if he had anything in his hand but each blow caused her to stop resisting.

She backed away from her old Mazda as the attacker got into the driver's seat. When the signal changed he drove off as she was left standing in the middle of the street with traffic buzzing by her. As she stood there all alone, she realized that she had better get out of the street before she was run over. She staggered over to the sidewalk. No one stopped to help her. She didn't want to follow the suspect's example of stopping cars by banging on their hoods when they stopped for the signal.

She turned around dejected and starting walking by herself several blocks to her house. There she called the police and told them what had happened. Shortly someone came to her house and took a report which included the description of her Mazda and her purse that had in it all her credit cards and identification.

Mary slowly tried to rethink her adventure and told herself that she was so lucky to be alive and not a victim of a rape or something more serious. True her face had some bruises from the blows she suffered, but those injuries would heal in time. Even though she was pleased that it wasn't worse all of a sudden she started thinking of all the places she had to call about her credit cards. What bothered her the most was the thought of having to go to her local DMV to obtain another driver's license. She hated standing in the long lines at the DMV just like everyone else did.

CHAPTER 7 INVESTIGATING THE CRASH SITE

As the LAPD field sergeant stood at the crash site, he thought to himself, "What the hell do we have here? Is this just a high-speed pursuit that ended in an accident? If so, the Traffic Division would handle that type of case. However, in this situation the police knew that the Bentley was stolen as part of a residential robbery. Then maybe the Robbery Division would handle the case. The key to this situation involved the identification of Christopher Rawlings.

Initially the police couldn't find any identification on the body of the male subject who appeared to have major head trauma. He was so severely injured that he couldn't talk and explain that he was a true victim of the robbery. The officers at the Rawlings house could only say that the husband of the house was missing. It wasn't until later that Lorie was told to go to the Northridge Hospital emergency room so she could identify the injured party. Much to her surprise the man with the crushed-in skull was her husband.

As soon as the police were able to put all the pieces together, they realized that they had a case of a Residential Robbery/Carjacking resulting in serious injuries. But that still didn't determine who should be assigned to lead the investigation on this case. The pivotal point revolved around Christopher's head injuries. This is one of the delicate decisions that the police officers have to make. If the victim of the residential robbery is likely to die then the assignment of the case is given to the Homicide team. However, if the victim is likely to recover then the Robbery detectives can handle the case.

The police sent someone over to the hospital to see if anyone would give a prognosis of the victim's injuries. No final answer could be made as to the extent of the trauma to the brain until the head X-rays had been completed. However, the police needed to know in general terms what the victim's chances were. When an informal inquiry was made to one of the ER nurses, she shook her head and uttered that she had never seen anyone recover from such fractures of the skull. The officer nodded a thank you to the nurse and walked outside the emergency room and found an empty hallway. He took his radio out of his belt and called the station to give them a 'heads up' as to the victim's condition. The officer told the station the bad news. The watch commander decided that this residential robbery should be handled as a homicide. Even though that wasn't a scientific medical decision at least it would put into motion which detectives should be working the case.

As a result, the homicide detail was notified that it was time for a call to action. The lucky or unlucky team that was next up was detectives Powell and Weston (Pseudonyms). They were notified that there was high likelihood that this 'Res Robbery' would turn into a homicide. These veteran detectives knew better than anyone that the first 48 hours were the most crucial time in solving a homicide as well as catching suspects. The best clues seem to evaporate the more time passes.

Both assigned detectives reluctantly left the comfort of their warm homes to brave the elements on this damp dreary night. They decide to divide up the investigative duties with several other detectives in order to get a handle on what they had. They assigned one group to the robbery crime scene at the house and the other group would respond to the crash site.

Detective Gaines (Pseudonym) drove to the crash site on Tampa Avenue and found yellow crime scene tape cordoning off the area. The detective with his partner walked over to the sergeant in charge and asked in a cynical voice, "What do we have here?"

The sergeant with a half-smile said, "This was the battle between the Bentley and the Tree and the Tree won." The sergeant started explaining in a typical Sgt. Joe

Friday monotone voice that there had been a short pursuit in which the Bentley struck a small Chevrolet and the Bentley went out of control ending up crashing into the sycamore tree.

He added that a male was injured who was later found near a wall and he had been transported to Northridge Hospital. Further the field sergeant said that the person had no identification on him but he might be the victim of the res-robbery or possibly one of the suspects. The sergeant mentioned that one of the officers talked to another driver who had come on the scene and that person saw what looked like a black male dressed in black climb out of the Bentley and take off running through the neighborhood.

The sergeant tried to assure the detectives that he had deployed officers throughout the neighborhood looking for the suspect or suspects. Since the searching of the area was proving to be productive, the sergeant directed the detectives to the open the driver's door of the Bentley. The sergeant used his flashlight to illuminate the once plush interior of the Bentley. The detectives started examining the interior looking for anything that could identify the possible suspects.

It wasn't long before they spotted a revolver on the passenger-side floorboard. With a pencil one of the detectives leaned the gun over to see if it was loaded. Since they wanted to preserve any possible fingerprints, he repositioned the gun as he had found it. The next item that caught the detectives' attention was what looked like a police scanner. They flipped it over to look to see if it was in the 'on' position and afterward flipped it back over.

As the detectives stood next to the open Bentley door, they noticed some type of clothing on the car seat and ground. Again, the one detective used his trusty pencil to lift up the item on the seat and as he stretched it out he could see that it was a ski mask. By then they had discovered that the other black item on the ground was also a ski mask. The one detective quipped to the other detective that these guys were true professionals. The other black item was determined to be a glove.

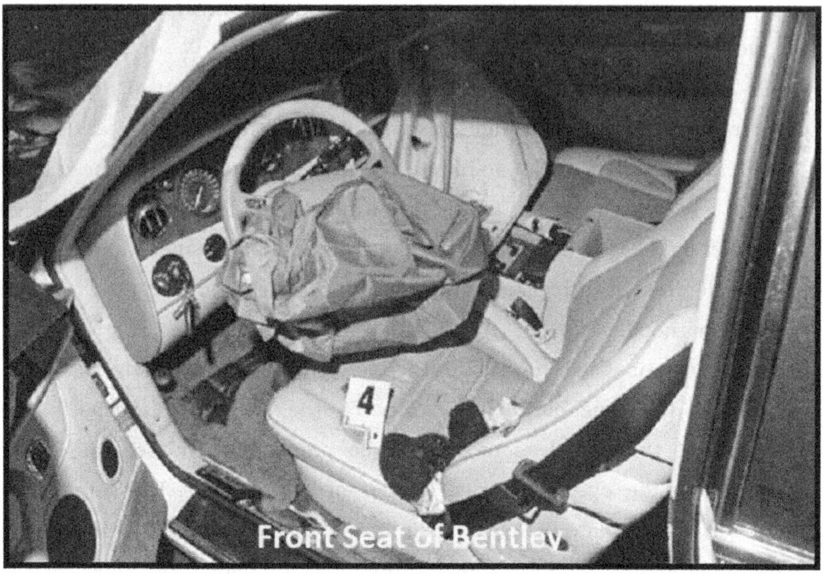

Front Seat of Bentley

Then the detective asked the sergeant if the person transported to the hospital had any gunshot wounds. The sergeant had a puzzled expression on his face. After some thought he said that he didn't recall the officers saying anything about gunshot wounds. The officers had only mentioned that the man's head appeared to be smashed in.

Handcuffs in Leaves

As an afterthought, the sergeant told the detectives that they needed to see one other strange thing. The sergeant motioned for the detectives to follow him. The three of them walked 50 feet to the northeast and stood near a cinder block wall. The sergeant directed his flashlight to a lower section on the wall. The detectives could clearly see blood stains and clump of human hair and scalp. The sergeant said that maybe that was where the injured person struck his head against the cinder block wall.

As the three of them were shining their flashlights around one of them said that he thought he saw a handcuff in the leaves under a bush. The one detective leaned over and took his pencil and picked up a white pair of handcuffs. He exclaimed that the hasps were open which seemed strange. The other detective stared at the handcuffs in disbelief. He turned to the sergeant and said that he would need a report from all the other officers on the scene to determine if they had lost a pair of handcuffs.

The detectives thanked the sergeant for the briefing and the detectives indicated that they would take over the crime scene investigation. The detectives made their own cursory inspection of the area. As they looked at the ground they saw what appeared to be a remote control opener for a garage door. They could see a streak of blood across the face of it. They placed it inside the trunk for later analysis.

As they walked across the grassy lawn they noticed grocery items strewn all over. Some of the groceries in glass containers were smashed open. When they looked into the backseat of the Bentley, they found paper bags with the name Fatburger which contained hamburgers and fries.

The detectives knew that the crash site investigation had to be completed before DWP could restore power to the area and the front yard turned back over to the property owner. The detectives gave all the assignments to the CSI team to take photos and collect the evidence and log it in. The major piece of evidence CLUE# 3 was the mangled Bentley and they directed the tow company to transport it to an impound lot under the control of the police authority.

CHAPTER 8 CHECKING OUT THE HOUSE

The lead detectives Powell and Weston decided to personally go to the Residential Robbery (Rawlings) house before going to the hospital. They wanted to check out what evidence needed to be collected as well as talk to anyone who was at the house at the time of the robbery. By the time the detectives arrived at the house it had yellow crime scene tape all around the front of the house. Since the street lights and electricity hadn't been affected in this area, the house was lit up like a Christmas gift ready to be placed under large Yuletide tree. The neighbors were standing in their front yards staring in the direction of the Rawlings house. They seemed to be in disbelief that anything sinister could happen in this small enclave thought to be one of the safest places in LA.

The detectives drove up to the yellow tape blocking the street and waved to one of the officers to lift up the tape so they could drive in and park closer to the house. As homicide detectives they hadn't spent much time in this area of Woodland Hills since this area was squeaky clean. Violent crime didn't happen here. However, this was an upscale area and should be easy pickings for burglars. All the houses had security systems which discouraged the professional burglars except for meth heads who were desperate for money and weren't concerned about being caught.

The detectives walked over to a group of officers near the front door. "Who can fill us in as to what happened?" One of the officers stepped forward indicating he had spoken to the wife. He explained that the wife had left for the hospital. But before she left she had showed him around the house pointing things out.

The detectives would have preferred getting a firsthand account of what happened but they were willing to listen to any information the officer could give them. The officer related that the wife's name was Lorie Rawlings and she and her husband lived together in this house with their two daughters. She started out by saying that she had been waiting for her husband to arrive with the food for dinner. Originally she heard the car pull into the garage but when her husband didn't bring in the food she went to the garage door to see what was holding him up. She related to the officer that was when she saw two males with ski masks pointing guns at her husband. That was when she stepped back into the kitchen and grabbed her portable phone and ran upstairs to gather up her children.

At that point the officer motioned to the detectives to come into the house so he could better explain what the wife had told him. The officer directed the detectives to follow him up the stairs where he pointed out where the wife and the children hid on the ledge outside on the roof. Then the officer directed the detectives to the master bedroom where he pointed to the dresser with a jewelry box on top. The detectives could see the drawers had been emptied out and they made a mental note to themselves that they needed to talk to the wife to get a complete description as to what was missing.

Then the detectives asked if the wife had provided a description of the robbers. The officer indicated that the wife claimed that the suspects were wearing dark clothing with ski masks covering their faces. The officer mentioned that she couldn't make out what race they were such as black, white or Hispanic. The best the wife came up with was that she thought she had seen part of one of the robber's hands and she thought it was light in color.

The only other time she got a look at the robbers was when they backing the Bentley out of the garage. Her vantage point for observing them was from the roof looking down on the top of the Bentley. The detectives thanked the officer for filling them in on what the wife had said. As they walked downstairs to the kitchen, the officer pointed to an orange container on the kitchen counter. The officer pointed to it and chuckled slightly. The wife had told him that the robbers had stopped during the robbery to take the orange container out of the refrigerator and drink from it. This fact amused the detectives and they made a note to have it saved as evidence.

The detectives had a basic understanding of what had happened and realized that they needed to interview Lorie to obtain a more complete description of the suspects as well as more details on the jewelry and property taken from the house. Since they knew she was at the hospital they could talk to her while she was waiting around to find out about the condition of her husband.

As the detectives were making notes about what the officer had told them, the forensic photographer had arrived at the house and the detectives went around pointing out what they wanted photographed. They didn't have to give too much direction to the photographer since this forensic photographer had taken pictures of hundreds of crime scenes and all she needed to know were the basic facts.

The detectives walked through the upstairs and explained to the photographer the importance of taking numerous photos of the infant's room especially outside the window. They left the photographer to do her job and headed back downstairs. They saw one of the CSI technicians and told him to collect the orange juice container and have it analyzed for latent prints.

As they finished up with the interior of the house they stepped outside and one of the officers said that he had seen some duct tape on the side of the house near the garage door. The detectives walked across the driveway and the officer walked over to some shrubs and pointed his flashlight on the ground. There was a large roll of duct tape. The one detective leaned down to get a closer look. He told the other detective to go back inside and ask the CSI guy to make sure to pick it up and take it as evidence.

The detective continued to use his own flashlight and spotted several shoe prints in the mud. Since it had recently rained the shoe prints seemed too wet to be of much value. At least it was worth taking photos of the muddy prints CLUE#4 and to make cast molds from Plaster of Paris (The term came from the King of France ordering that all wooden walls in Paris to be covered with plaster to protect them against fire.)

The two detectives got back together near the front door. They were told that Lorie was still at the hospital and they should immediately go there. With that the detectives quickly walked to their car and drove directly to the Northridge Hospital.

CHAPTER 9- HOSPITAL VISIT

The Northridge Hospital was like any suburban hospital. It was a beehive of activity during the day and tapers down to a ghostly place during the early morning hours. The detectives headed to the emergency room where the reception room was occupied by a 'slip and fall' victim and a young skateboarder who apparently had forgotten to wear his safety pads. The detectives told the receptionist that they were there to see the person who had been transported by ambulance from a car crash on Tampa Avenue.

The receptionist said that would be ER room #4. As the detectives walked back looking for #4 they could hear some sobbing coming from behind the curtain. At that moment the detectives didn't have to be told a thing. There 'Res Robbery' sounded like it may be turning into a HOMICIDE. The detectives didn't want to be intrusive but they had to find out if the person who was found at the crash site was Lorie's husband.

The doctors seemed to be preoccupied with trying to decide how to proceed with Christopher's treatment. The detectives not wanting to bother the doctors in their intense discussions went over to one of the nurses who was monitoring one of the IVs hooked to the victim. The one detective in a low almost a whisper asked how's the patient doing. The nurse didn't say anything but she shook her head uttering softly, "All we can do is pray." This was the second police officer who had approached her and she didn't want to get in trouble with the hospital administration by giving out personal medical information.

So she nodded her head in the direction of one of the emergency doctors who was writing something on a file. The detective walked over to the doctor who he had seen on other occasions. "Hi Doc how's it going?" The ER doctor looked at the detectives and seemed to recognize them. The detective cut to the chase, "How bad is the head injury?" Likewise, the doctor shook his head and said, "This guy must have hit something really hard since his skull is fractured into several pieces."

The detectives were trying to show some restraint and not seem too callous, but all they wanted to know was whether the victim was going to live or die. If the victim wasn't going to survive then it would become a full-fledged Homicide case which required a formal protocol. They felt a little ghoulish but they needed to know what type of investigation to plan for.

The other detective blurted it out, "What's his chances of making it?" The ER doc didn't want to sound negative but understood the reason for the question. He said, "All we can do is relieve the pressure on the brain and wait 24 hours to see if the swelling goes down." He admitted that the prognosis didn't look good but occasionally some patients do survive. The detectives thanked the ER doc and said they would be in contact with the hospital the next day to learn about the patient's condition.

Two days later on Wednesday, February 9, 1999, at 6:01 p.m. the doctor at the Northridge Hospital officially declared Christopher Rawlings dead from severe brain trauma. Thus began one of the most delicate parts of the investigation. The detectives needed an accurate description of the stolen items in order to put out an alert to the pawnshops to be on the lookout for the stolen jewelry and Rolex watches.

The only person who had knowledge about the stolen items was Lorie. The detectives were well aware that she was going through the most tragic days of her young life. Her husband was dead and she had to plan a funeral for him while tending to their two children. This was not the time to bother her for a description and serial numbers of the watches. However, the detectives know that stolen property is pawned almost immediately days after the crime. If the killers were to be caught, the detectives needed the information NOW CLUE# 4.

With the utmost diplomacy the detectives contacted Lorie and asked for the information and to their surprise Lorie went through some family files and obtained the information. As a result, the detectives had the following information:

Cartier bracelet & earring

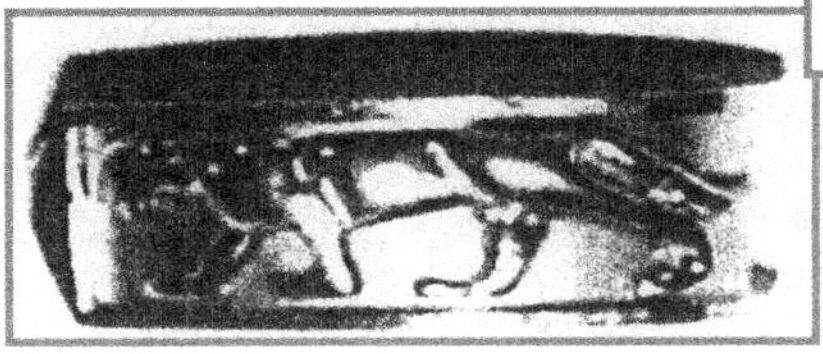

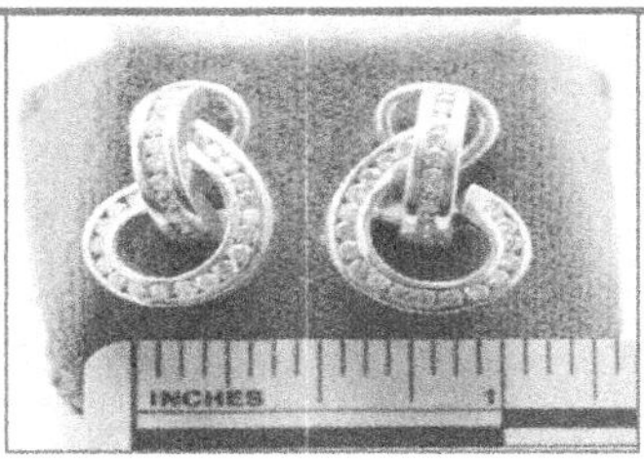

Presidential series Rolex watch and Blue Rolex watch

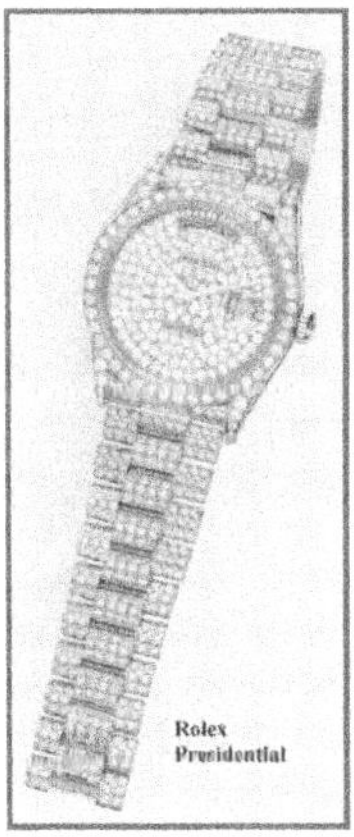

Also, taken by the robbers was a Swiss Army knife (This term was coined by American soldiers after World War II due to the difficulty they had in pronouncing "Offiziersmesser" the German name for the multi-purpose knife.) The detectives were pleased that this type of Swiss Army knife did contain a serial number. All these descriptions with the photos and serial numbers were distributed to local pawn shops.

CHAPTER 10 NEED A DESCRIPTION

Numerous LAPD officers and even dispatchers were trying to develop the best descriptions of the suspects they could from information coming in from various sources. The officers who were involved in the pursuit gave the description of the suspects as male blacks of average height and weight wearing black. Those officers added that one of the suspects appeared to be limping as he climbed out of the mangled Bentley.

On the night of the incident the watch commander on duty recognized that the physical description was so general that it would be of little use in tracking down the robbers. However, when he heard about one of the suspects limping, he thought that person might try to obtain medical assistance at one of the local hospitals. In order to be proactive the West Valley LAPD Division staff started calling the various hospitals and urgent care facilities to alert them to look out for someone who came in complaining of injuries from a traffic accident.

The police contacted the Kaiser Permanente Hospital and spoke to someone at the registration desk. They gave her a 'heads up' as to the type of person they were looking for. At 12:30 a.m. Elizabeth Williams (Pseudonym) was working the registration desk at the Kaiser Hospital when she received a call from a person who gave the name of 'Wilma' (Pseudonym). This individual asked if a Boris Graham or Jubba Pattis had been admitted to the hospital due to some type of traffic accident CLUE #6.

The receptionist, Williams, checked the records and didn't find anyone by that name. Next the caller asked if any black male had been admitted. The receptionist asked about the possible age of the person. The caller recited back 'March 3rd 1970' all in one breath. That impressed the receptionist since seldom does a caller know a patient's DOB. With that added information the receptionist again checked the log of patients and she told the caller that there was no one there with that DOB. Williams indicated she was sorry she couldn't find such a patient and the caller indicated that she would just keep calling the various hospitals to see if they had admitted a Boris Graham as a patient.

Boris Graham

After that conversation was completed the receptionist noticed that they had had such a patient Boris Graham DOB 3/3/70 on a previous occasion. Ms. Williams thought that had been a strange call and made some notes of the conversation. As she was thinking about the call she remembered that several hours earlier a LAPD officer had called about someone who might have been injured in a traffic accident. She recalled that the police were interested in a possible male black. She started comparing the descriptions and realized that might be the person the police were looking for. She contacted LAPD and gave them the information.

The information was passed on to the detectives. Although they were all very busy, one of them took the information and was able to find that the caller was Wilma Carson (Pseudonym) a female black residing in Van Nuys. On the next day at 5:15 p.m. they had tracked her down and interviewed her about making the phone call to Kaiser Hospital. She willingly admitted making the phone call looking for Boris Graham. She indicated that Boris sometimes babysat their children when she worked. She explained that Boris had originally gone by the name Jubba Pattis but had changed his name about four years earlier.

What seemed odd to the detectives was the fact that Wilma had no idea where Boris could be located even though the day before she had been calling all over looking for him. She confirmed that Boris didn't have a car and didn't have a job.

As to information about a Boris Graham, the detectives soon realized that they were wasting their precious time trying to track him down based on a hunch from a receptionist from the Kaiser Hospital. The detectives placed a 'flag' on the name Boris Graham in the police computer system and moved on to more promising leads.

It was February 9, 1999, the news media was giving extensive coverage to the Rawlings Residential Robbery story. As a result, the LAPD West Valley Division was being inundated with calls from the public on possible clues. The detectives had to sift through a stack of calls figuring out which ones required immediate attention.

A call came in from a Jack Mayes (Pseudonym) on Oxnard Street indicating he found a bunch of clothes lying in the street in front of his van. He didn't know if they had anything to do with the accident that knocked out the electric power for the area. Since his house was reasonably close to the crash site, Detective Weston returned his call and agreed to meet him. When the detective met him he walked the detective to the front of his van and pointed to the dark clothing CLUE # 7. The detective leaned down and with latex gloves on picked up what appeared to be a sweatshirt with dark knit gloves rolled up inside. Also, there was a piece of duct tape stuck to the front of the sweatshirt.

The detective thanked citizen Mayes for calling and indicated that they would take the clothing for further review. The detective had no idea if these were clothes from the suspects but to be on the safe side, the detective took the items and booked them with the thought they could sort this all out at a later date.

As the hectic day continued, at 5:00 p.m. a call came into the detective bureau from a Donna Colliers (Pseudonym) who resided on Tampa Avenue near the crash site. She said that she was driving on one of the side streets near Tampa when she saw a male black searching through the bushes on the West side of the street. She used the word that the man seemed to be 'frantically' looking for something. What was strange was that a car was parked in the street while the man continued to look in the shrubbery.

The Detective Powell asked whether she had been able to get a good look at the person. She replied that she thought she had and described him as male black clean-shaven, close-cropped hair, around 6' tall and somewhere between 25 to 30 years of age, a medium build and wearing a leather jacket CLUE #8. The detective had to chuckle to himself since most civilians have difficulty providing any type of accurate description. However, Miss Colliers had supplied a detailed description. He had to think that this was the type of person that LAPD should be recruiting to be a police officer.

Then he thought he would test her knowledge of the car she saw him get into. He asked for a description of the car. To his surprise Miss Colliers fired back that the car was a tan over green convertible sports car like a Mustang CLUE #9. She apologized for not getting the license number even though she had tried to follow it. The Detective Powell thought that this most likely was useless information but since she was so thorough on her description of the person he asked if someone from LAPD could meet with her.

Kirell's Girlfriend's Mustang

Detective Weston was sent to meet with this witness. They met within an hour at the location she had seen the guy looking for something in the bushes. She directed the detective to the shrubbery on the parkway on the West side of the street. As the detective started searching the area he had to think that this was a futile search for a 'needle in a haystack' (Expression credited to St. Thomas More in 1532 who wrote, to seek out one line in a book would be like looking for a needle in a meadow). The detective didn't know what he was looking for. Could it be a gun or some money or piece of paper? The detective had to be thinking why he was spending his time on such a wild goose chase.

To appear appreciative of this witness, Donna Colliers, the detective continued to tread through the bushes. He had his eyes searching for anything out of the ordinary. Then by his left foot he saw something and pulled back on the bush covering it. All he could make out was something dark in color that looked like leather. He leaned down and picked up what turned out to be a wallet. He immediately flipped it open to see if it had any identification in it.

The Detective Weston's face lit up with a smile as he saw the name Christopher Rawlings. He further examined it, and could see money in it with several credit cards tucked into various pockets. He wanted to yell BINGO or EUREKA we have found it. The flush of excitement was brought back to reality thinking what did this wallet really prove. As the detective was processing the meaning of the wallet, he thought that the person who was looking for it might be one of the robbery suspects. Donna Colliers claimed that she could identify the person. Also, she had given the detective a detailed description of the car. Yet even with a good description of a person and of a car, how useful was all of this information?

The detective didn't want to take advantage of this civilian's willingness to get involved. The detective thanked her for helping them out and made an 'off the cuff' (Dinner speakers would write last minute ideas on their cuffs to remind them what to say) request. He asked her if she saw another car like the one the guy got into, to give him a call. On the following day the detective received another call from Donna Colliers and she said that she saw a similar car in the parking lot at the mall. She indicated that she had the license number of that similar car.

The detective in disbelief wrote it down and thanked her again. The detective told his partner that they needed to clone Donna Colliers. If all citizens were as cooperative as Donna the detectives thought what a wonderful world it would be. It would be like living next door to Mr. Roger when he would say, "Won't you be my neighbor?"

The detective gave the license number to a fellow detective to track it down. They went to the registered owner's house and took a photo of the car. As a result, they had a photo of a green 1997 Mustang with a tan convertible top, even though they weren't certain how it all fit together and what it meant.

CHAPTER 11- GETTING A GOOD DESCRIPTION

Immediately after the car crash the suspects ran in different directions. The first description came from Dani Yacovone (Pseudonym) who saw the suspects climb out of the car and take off running. The next set of descriptions came from all the residents in the area who saw the suspects climb over fences and run through backyards. Some of these residents were able to get a good look at the escaping robbers and were able to provide a description to the police. Even those who were confronted by a person banging on their car were also able to give a detailed description of that individual.

The detectives assigned the Rawlings case agreed to consolidate all the descriptions into one which could be put out in an all-points bulletin. However, when all the descriptions were distilled into one official description the detectives ended up with a male, black, between 20 and 30 who was of medium size and weight and wearing dark clothes CLUE #10.

The detectives looked at each other and not a word had to be spoken. This was like playing with dynamite. They knew that the ACLU would be all over them if they put out such a description as probable cause to arrest someone. These detectives had been around the block and knew that general descriptions often were practically useless. But they realized that they wanted to compile a list of all those who had given descriptions so when they did come up with possible suspects they knew who to show photo line-ups to.

Finding an easy way to solve a homicide is what every detective hopes for. The danger is that the easy way may not truly lead to the actual killer. That is why most veteran homicide detectives know that the old gumshoe approach by checking everything out thoroughly is the only way to investigate a homicide. Early on in the investigation of the Rawlings case, the lead detective received a phone call from an FBI agent who indicated that LAPD should talk to one of the FBI informants. Three days after the Rawlings incident the FBI agent came over to LAPD to explained that FBI had been investigating Christopher Rawlings for a possible telemarketing fraud scheme.

This revelation seemed a little out of character for what the detectives had uncovered about Christopher. Since the LAPD detectives hadn't come up with any solid suspects in the first 48 hours of the investigation, they were anxious to hear any viable suggestions as to possible suspects. Shortly thereafter the LAPD detective met with an FBI informant who explained that two of Christopher's associates in the fraud scheme were the two who killed him. The detective listen intently to the informant and everything he said seemed to add up. The detective obtained photos of the two business associates who had been mentioned.

Immediately the detective put together a photo line-up CLUE # 11 and started the arduous process of contacting all the possible eyewitnesses from the crash site. He showed the line-ups to everyone and not one person could identify either of the associates as the suspects in the Rawlings case. The Rawlings detectives had high hopes that the FBI was handing them the killers on a silver platter. However reality set in and the detectives weren't surprised that no usable information was obtained. These weathered detectives were well aware of how quick solutions can be nothing more than 'quicksand' for them to sink into. About two weeks later one of the detective received a call from an LAPD detective from another Division. This detective said that he had a reliable informant who the Rawlings detective should talk to. This informant claimed CLUE # 12 he had inside information on the 'Bentley Guy Killing.'

The Rawlings detectives were leery but agreed to meet with that informant named Leonard Shidler (Pseudonym) who was in custody on burglary charges. The detectives met him in the Van Nuys courthouse lock-up. This informant indicated that the brains behind the Rawlings killing was a Ken Kaplan (Pseudonym) who was an associate or friend of Christopher Rawlings. He further explained that one of the robbers was a Donald Tran (Pseudonym). The informant said that Donald admitted to being involved and had used the money he had obtained from the robbery to purchase new tires for his truck.

Now with these two names the detectives thanked the informant and immediately obtained a booking photo of Donald Tran. The detectives prepared a photo line-up and started showing it to the various witnesses who had seen the suspects. Mary who was the woman carjacked viewed the line-up. She nodded her head and pointed to the photo of Donald Tran and tentatively identified him. Other witnesses indicated that Donald's photo looked familiar but they weren't certain.

The detectives were in a quandary. Since witnesses were tentatively identifying someone, should they concentrate on this new information? The lead detective called up Christopher's brother Doug Rawlings and asked if he knew whether his brother was somehow associated with a person named Ken Kaplan. Christopher's brother said that he was very close to his brother and had never heard his brother mention a Ken Kaplan.

The detectives all gathered in the detective bureau and assessed the information they had received from this Leonard Shidler. One of the old time detectives had a more jaundiced view of informants. He reminded the other detectives that everything the informant had told them about the incident was information that had been mentioned by the news media. The only new thing added was the name of the so-called suspect, Donald Tran.

The lead detective didn't want to walk away from someone giving names of suspects. This detective decided that they would talk to the informant one more time. The next day the detective met with the informant again in the Van Nuys lock-up room. The detective didn't mince words and told the informant that his information didn't add up. There was a moment of silence as the informant sat there. Then a smile came over the informant's face. The detective knew they had been conned by the informant. The detective didn't want to stand up and leave since he was afraid that he might punch the informant in the mouth. After the informant was taken away, the detective returned to the station.

This wasn't the first time the detective had been burned by an informant. All he could think about was the amount of time that was wasted trying to verify the informant's information. Again the easy solution didn't seem to pan out and frustration and disappointment were setting in.

There was another approach and that was to piggyback their investigation on top of another investigation of a Residential robbery that occurred a week earlier before the Rawlings robbery. On January 31, 1999, just after midnight a Daniel Berg (Pseudonym) was asleep in his bedroom at his house in Sherman Oaks CLUE # 13. This location was approximately three miles east of the Rawlingses' house. Mr. Berg was awakened by two masked intruders armed with revolvers. The gunmen demanded property and when Mr. Berg hesitated the one robber struck him in the face with the gun.

The suspects wanted anything of value. They took two Rolex watches and two televisions and money from the victim's wallet. The robbery was quick and the masked men disappeared into the night. Needless to say, the victim wasn't able to provide a very useful description except they were males all dressed in black. The Berg robbery was assigned to the Robbery detectives who started putting out a description of the Rolex watches to the various pawn shops in the area.

The detectives in the Rawlings case were hoping that the Berg robbery detectives would be able to give them some leads. This was wishful thinking since the Berg detectives had nothing to show for all the investigation they had conducted. As a matter of fact the Berg detectives were pleased that the Rawlings case had come along so they could dovetail behind the homicide detectives.

The Rawlings detectives were beginning to feel the pressure from the news media making daily inquiries as to who had been arrested in the Rawlings killing. These detectives realized that the Rawlings case wasn't going to be solved quickly so they might as well get ready for a long and arduous investigation.

CHAPTER 12 - INVESTIGATION 101

What evidence was recovered at the Rawlings house? The answer was not much. They had recovered the orange juice container **CLUE #14** that one of the suspects may have drunk from. They had the crime lab dust the house and garage for latent prints. This was a long shot since there was evidence the robbers were wearing gloves. What made it more impracticable was the fact that the orange juice container had condensation on the outside of the container which interfered with any latent prints sticking to the surface. Needless to say nothing of value was found.

The next item from the house that was of marginal value was the photos of the shoe prints on the side of the house. These photos of the various shoe prints weren't useful since the police hadn't recovered any shoes to compare them to. At this stage the shoe prints weren't going to reveal who the robbers were.

The only other piece of evidence from the house was Lorie's description of the jewelry and watch that she found to be missing. There were other items missing from Christopher's personal property that included another Rolex, a gold bracelet and some money. The detectives asked Lorie if she had serial numbers for the two Rolex watches. She went through the old receipts and was able to come up with the serial numbers on both watches.

As to the pieces of jewelry, Lorie was able to come up with photos of the unique bracelet. Although the bracelet didn't have a serial number to identify it, at least it had been a part of a very limited number of bracelets that were created and sold at the Cartier Jewelry stores. What was so distinctive about the bracelet was the leaping

Jaguar design. Likewise the earrings that were stolen also contained the same Jaguar design.

The Rolex watches and jewelry that were taken would be only useful if the items were pawned or found in the possession of a suspect. At least this clue was a long shot but could prove to be crucial once a suspect was found.

The detectives turned their attention to the items found at the car crash site. One of the items was a police scanner CLUE # 15. The detectives had the CSI unit thoroughly examine the scanner for a serial number. They were able to find a serial number as well as a manufacturer number and determined that it was sold by Uniden Company in Fort Worth, Texas. This seemed promising. One of the detectives called the company and they were able to confirm that they manufactured and sold that particular scanner. However, the company didn't record what dealer it was sent to. All they could say was that they had three intermediate distributors in the Los Angeles area. Each one of those distributors had no records as to who they sold the scanners to.

The detectives' next move was to contact the manufacturer of the HWC handcuffs CLUE #16. These HWC handcuffs came from a company in Hyde Park, New York. When they were contacted they checked their files and found that they had eight distributors in the Los Angeles area. Although the handcuffs had serial numbers, neither the HWC nor any of their distributors recorded who they sold the handcuffs to. This information was the most that the detectives learned about that type of handcuff. All that the company said was that generally their handcuffs were sold to security guards or security companies since it was an inexpensive design.

The one piece of evidence that the detectives were counting on was the history on the revolver CLUE #17 that was found on the floor mat of the Bentley. This could be crucial in solving this case. Often guns recovered from a crime scene can reveal whether they had been used in other crimes or were a community weapon used by a particular gang.

To the shock of the detectives this gun didn't come back as a stolen or a weapon used in other crimes. The gun came back registered to Roy Harris (Pseudonym) who gave his home address as Riverside, California. The detectives soon realized from contacting Mr. Harris' family that he had passed away in 1996. A relative by the name of Rosie Rogers (Pseudonym) advised the detectives that the gun's whereabouts was unknown. To Rosie's recollection a group of guns owned by Mr. Harris were taken by his daughter Lony Peters (Pseudonym) who lived in Twin Falls, Idaho. The detectives contacted her and she admitted obtaining a number of her father's guns, but didn't have any knowledge on that specific revolver.

However, when one of the detectives was talking to her she made an off-handed comment about one of the other relatives. She said that she thought that her stepmother's grandson, a John Rogers (Pseudonym), had taken the gun. This statement intrigued the detectives and they followed up by asking why she thought he had the gun. She fired back that John was a narcotics user and a thief. She gratuitously added that she wouldn't be surprised if he sold the gun for drugs. All of a sudden dirty family secrets were being aired in public.

Naturally the detective had to follow up on what she had said. The detective tracked down John Rogers and asked him if he ever had his grandfather's revolver. He claimed he didn't have the gun but remembered that he had it back in 1995 but returned it to his grandfather's motorhome. When he was asked what he thought might have happened to the revolver he blamed it on Lony Peters. He claimed Lony ransacked the motorhome after Mr. Harris' death and took that revolver with other guns.

The revolver in the Bentley which had great potential in solving the Rawlings case now wasn't going to reveal any suspect.

The other items recovered in or near the Bentley was a knitted glove. Nothing of evidentiary value was going to be discovered from this glove. However, the two ski masks CLUE # 18 by themselves didn't seem to be worth much since they didn't have any serial number or identifiable features. Detective Gaines directed the CSI technician to photograph the ski masks and bag them for evidence just in case they became relevant in the case.

The only other forensic item that the detectives had from the crash site was the remote control for the garage opener. What was interesting about that item was that there appeared to be a blood smear across the face of the controls CLUE # 19. One of the detectives had found it on the ground near the back of the Bentley. He had picked it up and placed it in the trunk of the Bentley so it could be preserved. Later it was removed from the trunk and sent to the crime lab for analysis. When the DNA report came back it showed that the blood smear was from Christopher Rawlings which didn't yield any DNA evidence pointing to any suspects.

The crash site and Rawlings house crime scene weren't yielding any workable clues. To everyone's surprise, the lady who was carjacked near the crash site had some new information. Mrs. Vargas' son-in-law called the detectives and explained that Mrs. Vargas was notified that her debit card had been used. It was one of the cards taken from her purse at the time of the carjacking. The bank had notified her that her card was used at a Chevron service station in South Los Angeles. This was a long shot but possibly the person using her debit card could be identified CLUE#20. Detective Gaines was assigned to check out who might have used her debit card.

CHAPTER 13- *AMERICA'S MOST WANTED* TV PROGRAM

The news media was fascinated about the Rawlings story. Was it the fact that the crooks stole an expensive Bentley vehicle and crashed it into a power pole? Or, was the novelty, the fact that Lorie heroically protected her children by climbing out on a roof while calling 9-1-1? Or was it the fact that the husband was killed when he flew out of the trunk of a Bentley? It wasn't surprising that the TV program *America's Most Wanted* within a month was doing a re-enactment of the Rawlings case. That segment aired on April 3, 1999, and the viewers were asked to call if they had any information about the case or the missing Presidential Rolex watch that had been taken from the victim.

Such programs can often help solve cases, however most of the time it brings crazies out of thc woodwork who think they know something. Often the callers just want to be noticed and may be seeking their 15 seconds of fame. Sometimes the airing of a segment gets people thinking and it may take months before they decide to act and contact the police.

A little more than a month after the airing of the program on May 19, 1999, at 1:05 p.m. the lead detective's voice mail recorded the following message CLUE # 21:

"Hello, Detective Powell. At the address 13249 Vaughn Street in the City of Pacoima and the name is "Key-Rail. That's the person who kidnapped and stole that car, that Bentley, that

poor guy that died. You can pick him up there today. He's wearing a Maliah suit if you want him. Looks like Mohammed or something like that. Check it out."

Was this call generated by the TV segment? No one will ever know for sure since it was never determined who made the phone call. The detectives didn't know what to make of this call but they were appreciative of having the name "Key-Rail" and an address in Pacoima. The detective checked the gang database for the name but nothing came up anything close to "Key-Rail." This was disappointing but the detective decided to check out the address that was mentioned in the voice message. They found that the homeowner was a Betty Taylor (Pseudonym). She was an older black lady who had no criminal record.

Since the detectives were batting zero as to finding a suspect, on June 2, 1999, the lead detective with his partner got in their detective Crown Vic car (for years the police used Ford Crown Victorias) and drove to the address on Vaughn Street. They didn't want to tip off any suspect who might be at the location.

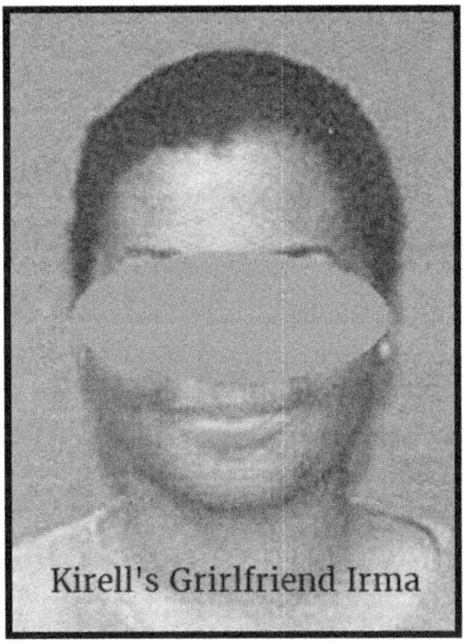

Kirell's Grirlfriend Irma

As the detectives slowly drove by the residence, they noticed a Mustang parked directly in front of the address CLUE# 22. What caught their attention about the convertible Mustang was that it was green in color with a tan top matching the exact description given to the police by Donna Colliers. She was the witness who saw someone frantically looking for something in the bushes near the crash site.

The two detectives looked at each other in disbelief. They turned around and drove back by the Mustang while one of them copied down the license plate number 3WHN236. When they got back to the station, they ran that number through the DMV database and it came back registered to an Irma Boulins (Pseudonym).

The detectives were feeling good in that they had a name to follow up on. They checked the name Irma Boulins through DMV driver's license and found that she gave her residence address as an address in Gardena. At that point the detectives had a location where they could find and talk to Miss Boulins. Again, their hopes were dashed when they found out that the address was only a post office box.

Out of frustration they set up a surveillance team to watch the Pacoima address of Betty Taylor. Without a doubt this seemed to be a useless exercise. The team never saw the Mustang return to the Vaughn Street residence. To occupy the team's time they started writing down license plate numbers of cars parked in front of the residence.

They related that information to the detectives at the station. One of the license plate numbers came back to a Jabali Lavell Davis (Pseudonym) who was on parole. The detectives didn't know what they had if anything. They called the San Fernando Valley Office of the California State Parole Board to ask about Jabali Davis. They didn't find anything useful about that individual.

During that conversation the detectives mentioned they were checking out the Vaughn Street address. The person at the parole office said that she would run that address to see if they had any information about it. About 30 seconds later the parole officer came back on the line and said the only information on that address was that a parolee by the name of Kirell Francis Taylor once resided there with his grandmother Betty Taylor.

Maybe it was the way the parole officer pronounced the parolee's name "Kirell" that the detectives wanted to hear "Key-Rail." This piqued the detectives' interest and they asked if they could get more information on him. The parole officer pulled up the file on Kirell Taylor and explained that he was married to Irma Boulins who drove a green Mustang convertible.

The detectives weren't coming up with a location to find Kirell Taylor so the detectives concentrated on the whereabouts of Irma Boulins. They ran the Mustang for possible tickets and came up with another address for Miss Boulins in Torrance. The detectives went to that address and found it to be a large apartment house. They went to the manager's office and asked about a possible Irma Boulins living there sometime in the past.

The manager was cooperative and pulled up the old rental agreement document. The detectives by this time had a photo of Miss Boulins and showed it to the manager who immediately said, "That's her." They asked if anyone else resided with her and she said that she thought that she had a boyfriend. The detectives showed the manager a photo of Kirell Taylor and she nodded and said, "That's him."

It was strange how information started out as an anonymous tip of the name "Key Rail" and an address in Pacoima and ended up turning the corner of the case. However, the detectives were a long way from solving the case.

LAPD floated the name Kirell Taylor among other law enforcement agencies to see if anyone was investigating that person on some other crime. To the detectives' surprise Hawthorne Police Department had an active investigation on Kirell Taylor for a take-over robbery. The LAPD detectives met with the Hawthorne detectives to learn about their investigation.

They were told that on March 12, 1999, a car agency on Prairie Avenue in Hawthorne was robbed CLUE # 23. A robber, later identified as Eric Sterling (Pseudonym), entered the offices of the car agency with a gun and immediately blindfolded the two employees. Then the robber took money from the cash register and some keys from cars in the lot. While the robber was busy taking items one of the employees was able to reach a phone and dialed 9-1-1. Before he was able to say anything to the operator the robber came back over to the blindfolded victims. The salesman was able to discreetly place the receiver down on a table.

As a result, the 9-1-1 operator was able to hear the robbery taking place and dispatched police units. The robber didn't notice the phone on the table. He continued to talk to someone on a two-way radio and told that person that the location had been cleared. Shortly thereafter another person came into the office and talked to the robber.

The robber Eric Sterling went out and got into the passenger side of a Dodge Intrepid which was registered to him. The car sped off from the car agency followed by the responding police units. Several blocks away the passenger Eric Sterling jumped out of the car. Officer stopped and went into foot pursuit of Sterling and eventually caught him.

It was not until the next day did the police locate the abandoned Dodge Intrepid. When they conducted a search of the Dodge, they found in the trunk a wallet in a pair of boots. When they examined the wallet, it contained the identification of Kirell Taylor.

CHAPTER 14- ZEROING IN ON TAYLOR

The Hawthorne detectives indicated that they had filed robbery charges against Eric Sterling. However they were trying to connect Kirell Taylor to the takeover robbery of the car agency but hadn't had an opportunity to talk to Taylor. It was agreed by both the Hawthorne detectives and LAPD detectives Powell and Weston to ask Lynn Morris (Pseudonym) who was the parole officer assigned Kirell Taylor to have him come into the Parole Office so these two sets of detectives could talk to him.

On July 13, 1999, Taylor's parole officer arranged to have Kirell come over to the Parole Office CLUE # 24. In order to gain Kirell's cooperation she had only told him that she wanted to talk to him about updating information about where he was living and working. To Kirell it seemed like a typical parole meeting which he knew how to bullshit his way through it. He felt that he was such a good talker that he would be able to get himself out of there in less than an hour.

Little did Kirell realize as he walked into the parole officer's office, that he would never walk another step as a 'free man' for the rest of his life. Kirell must have thought it was strange that his parole officer's office was a wee bit crowded. But he wasn't concerned since he could handle anything. He immediately sat down next to his parole officer's desk and projected the appearance of a dude who was on top of the world.

The parole officer stood up and walked over behind Kirell. She said in a matter of fact voice, "Kirell I am taking you into custody. Put your hands behind you." All of a sudden it was like a hibernating bear had awakened. Kirell jumped out of the chair and took a combative stance with his clenched fists in front of him. He yelled out, "This is the way it's going to be! I ain't going nowhere!" He refused to comply with the orders to submit to an arrest. He exclaimed he wasn't going anywhere with anyone.

Then he began shouting "I ain't going to Van Nuys court and be wrongfully accused of something that I didn't do." At that point the Hawthorne detective stepped forward and looked at Kirell and said, "I'm not taking you to Van Nuys court but to Inglewood court instead." Kirell's immediate response was, "For What?" The Hawthorne detective advised him it was for robbery. What shocked everyone in the parole office was that Kirell all of sudden placed his fists in front of him to be handcuffed. Kirell's only statement was "Oh, well, I ain't done no robbery. You can take me to jail. You'll find out that I ain't done no robbery in Inglewood."

The two LAPD detectives from the Rawlings case didn't feel slighted by the fact he didn't seem to want to go to their Van Nuys court. Both of them remained silent and let the Hawthorne detective do all the talking because they had a viable case against Kirell. The parole officer instructed Kirell that he had to give a blood sample which he willingly did. The LAPD detectives obtained Kirell's blood and took it to the station where they booked it as evidence. Kirell's blood sample would become highly relevant later in the case.

The Rawlings detectives were riding high since they at least had the name of a person of interest. The only thing that the detectives had was that an anonymous caller had said that a person by the name of "Key-Rail" was involved in the Bentley case. They had focused in on a Kirell Taylor who appeared to be involved in a take-over robbery in Hawthorne.

At that point LAPD didn't have any evidence they could use in court to prove that Kirell was one of the robbery suspects in the Rawlings case. But the detectives knew it was time to ramp up their investigation. They started by preparing a photo line-up which included Kirell's photo that would be shown to the various eyewitnesses. When they showed the photo line-up to Mary Vargas, who was attacked by the suspect and dragged out of her car, she said, "Number 4 looks like the man that stole my car." The number 4 photo was of Kirell Taylor and this was a big boost for the detectives.

When the detectives contacted Connie Lozano, Oren Aaron and David Mark they received the same response. They all indicated that number 4 looked similar to the person they observed running from the crash site. Some of the other eyewitnesses picked out Kirell as well as another person as the possible suspects. They were able to find Donna Colliers who had seen the person the next day hunting through the bushes and showed her the photo line-up. However, her identification was of another individual and not Kirell.

After all the eyewitnesses had been shown the photo line-up the detectives regrouped. They could quickly see that the eyewitnesses were okay but any Defense attorney could easily attack the identification in court. The witnesses mainly said that it looked like Kirell but no absolute 100% identification.

It became obvious that the detectives needed stronger evidence to connect Kirell to the Rawlings robbery and killing. Now they had good evidence as to where Kirell lived. The hope was maybe he still had some incriminating evidence where he lived. Since it was now August, six months from the time of the crime, it was less likely that such evidence still existed.

On August 17, 1999, the detectives prepared and obtained a search warrant for 13249 Vaughn Street in Pacoima where Kirell had been living with his grandmother. That morning before the detectives could execute the search warrant they received a phone call from Kirell in a three-way call with his aunt.

Kirell was upset with the detectives and said, "Why did you take my blood several weeks ago. You took it illegally since I didn't know you were investigating me in the robbery murder of Christopher Rawlings." It was a strange conversation for him to have with the detectives in the case. Apparently in Kirell's mind he believed that the police are required to inform him of any possible crime they are investigating him for. The detectives were on their way out the door of the police station to execute a search warrant for his residence, so they told him they were in a hurry but they could talk about the blood sample at some later time.

By the time the detectives arrived at his grandmother's house in Pacoima it was 10:30 a.m. They knocked on the door to give notice that they were there to execute a search warrant. No one came to the door but they could hear music coming from the back of the premises so they went to the rear of the house. There was a living unit next to the garage where they came into contact with a Shalo Taylor. They asked her where Kirell's bedroom was located and she pointed to the main house. She said it was the southwest bedroom.

The detectives returned to the main house and entered the described bedroom. To confirm that it was Kirell's bedroom, they found photos of him and his girlfriend on the dresser. Also there were numerous letters with Kirell Taylor's name on them. The two main detectives looked at each other and without saying a word knew this was their big opportunity to find any incriminating evidence if it existed. One of the detectives went to the east side of the room and started meticulously searching for anything that could connect Kirell to the Rawlings case.

The other detective started on the other side of the room next to the bed. His eyes noticed a small basket on the nightstand. For months that detective had on his desk, photos of Lorie's missing earrings and bracelet from Cartier. He had hoped that they would show up at some pawn shop. Those two pieces of stolen jewelry had been etched into his mind. As his eyes fixated on this little basket he saw something his mind recognized. He couldn't believe his eyes. There was one of Lorie's earrings CLUE # 25. It was quite unique made of yellow metal, with an open loop and a single Jaguar jungle cat in a walking posture between the edges of the loop.

He wanted to yell bingo but he realized this wasn't the appropriate place to celebrate the big break in the case. Just like the happy fisherman who made the big catch he immediately started looking for another big one to reel in. In this case the detective started fishing around in the little basket looking for the other earring. There was a lot of junk in the basket but no additional earring.

Although there was disappointment in not finding the other earring, this setback was erased when all of a sudden the detective spotted Lorie's bracelet under items on the nightstand. Now two items had been positively identified as being stolen from Lorie's jewelry box which had been on her bedroom dresser. The case against Kirell had improved greatly.

The other detective had worked his way into Kirell's closet and found a pair of Nike running shoes size 8 ½. Since they had plaster casts of shoe prints from the crash site, the detective picked up the shoes and took them for comparison at the crime lab.

The other big find in Kirell's bedroom was when they located a Koran at the foot of his bed. When they looked at the Koran it contained a business card from Rodney

Leonard of Gentleman's Quarters. This became CLUE # 26 which was the type of evidence that doesn't prove that Kirell actually committed the crime, however the inference is that Kirell had some type of contact with Christopher's business. This is the type of evidence that forces a defendant at trial to take the witness stand to explain the damning evidence.

Through extensive investigation the detectives had discovered that Kirell's girlfriend was Irma Boujourx CLUE #27 who was living on Via Verde Street in Palmdale. After they finished the search of the Pacoima house they headed to Palmdale in the Mojave Desert. This was a city that had experienced big booms and severe bust depending on the aircraft manufacturing business of Southern California.

The search of Miss Boujourx's residence didn't prove to be fruitful for the Rawlings case. It appeared that Kirell's girlfriend had moved on with her life after he was arrested and taken into custody. While searching this Palmdale location the detectives came across numerous items for fraudulent driver's licenses and evidence of possible welfare fraud. The detectives recognized that all this incriminating evidence had nothing to do with Kirell. While conducting their search Irma Boujourx drove up in her green convertible Mustang and the detectives explained to her they were conducting a search warrant of her apartment.

Since the search warrant included her Mustang, one of the detectives started looking through the interior of the Mustang but came up with nothing useful. However, when he started searching the trunk of the Mustang he noticed a traffic citation. He picked it up in order to examine it and noticed that the citation was made out to Kirell Taylor while driving this Mustang. Although this wasn't highly incriminating, it did provide proof that Kirell did in fact drive this Mustang vehicle. This corroborated Miss Collier's statement who claimed she saw a black male driving a green Mustang convertible who was frantically looking for something in the bushes.

Miss Boujourx was detained as they continued the search. After finding all the fraudulent identification she was arrested and taken into custody. When she was interviewed by the detectives she waived her Miranda Rights and denied any involvement in the Rawlings case. She admitted that she had lived with Kirell several months ago.

On the next day August 8, 1999, the detectives felt they had enough evidence to sit down with defendant Kirell Taylor and get his side of the case. This would be CLUE # 28 if he was willing to confess to the detectives. They met Kirell at the main County Jail and advised him of his Miranda rights, which he said he was willing to waive. But when they started asking questions about the Rawlings case, it was like a total disconnect. Kirell shook his head and said that he had not been involved in that crime nor had he ever been in the Bentley that crashed. Then he changed his tune and said he didn't want to talk without having an attorney present. At that point the detectives closed up their notebooks, stood up and left.

The detectives would have liked to obtain a confession from Taylor. But most of all they would have liked him to divulge who his partner in crime was. They were realistic enough to know that sometimes things don't fall into place.

When they had the eyewitnesses look at the photo line-ups including Kirell, the detectives decided to have the two ski masks examined by the LAPD Scientific Investigation Division. The hope was that the crime lab could obtain sufficient cellular material such as sweat and saliva from the ski masks which could be analyzed to determine if the DNA matched Kirell's. Even though the DNA test took considerable time, it was worth waiting for. The DNA on the ski mask #3 came back as a match to Kirell with a frequency of 1 in 335,100 individuals. That was something to be jubilant about. Yet the detectives would have liked it better if the other ski mask #4 had come back with a match to some other suspect listed in the DNA database.

At this stage in the investigation one of Sherlock Holmes' infamous quotes from the book *The Beryl Coronet* seemed relevant that being, "It is an old maxim of mine that when you have excluded the impossible, whatever remains, however improbable, must be the truth."

The detectives returned to their office at the West Valley Division and assembled all their reports so they could submit the case to the filing deputy at the Van Nuys DA's Office. By the end of the day the detectives had a formal felony complaint against Kirell Taylor for the following charges:

1. Murder
2. Kidnapping to commit a robbery
3. Kidnapping to commit carjacking

4. Robbery
5. First Degree Burglary
6. Carjacking
7. Evading an officer causing death

Kirell who was now 24 years old was arraigned on the charges and shortly thereafter he was giving interviews to the local newspaper. Kirell stated the following:

"I'm definitely innocent, and I've been framed by the police department in West Valley. I have no idea why. I guess I fit the MO. I felt if O.J. could be accused, anyone can, and I never thought in a million years it would be me. I'm innocent....

On the night of the Rawlings robbery and wild police chase, I was relaxing at home with my family watching TV....

I don't create heinous acts like that. I'm not a Jeffrey Dahmer nor North Hollywood robbery bandits. I'm Kirell a loving, compassionate individual. I definitely want my day in court."

It was unclear why he was talking to the news media and how his remarks were going to be helpful to him.

CHAPTER 15- TAYLOR'S TRIAL

Kirell thought well of himself and his 'gangster smarts' may have blinded him to reality. Needless to say his trial took on a circus-like atmosphere. What was his strategy for winning his trial in front of a jury? Since he was indigent the court was required to provide him with an attorney who would represent him in all the court proceedings. One attorney was appointed to represent him but Kirell didn't like his lack of aggressiveness. The court appointed another attorney and Kirell wasn't pleased with him either.

Over a two-year period, Kirell went through a half dozen attorneys none of which he felt had sufficient knowledge of DNA. As he put it, his case fundamentally rested on the DNA evidence found on the ski mask. He felt he needed a Defense attorney who was up to date on the latest DNA issues in order to create some doubt about the DNA analysis. Kirell finally was appointed an attorney who had the experience he felt was necessary to litigate his case.

Several months later that attorney was removed since he had some type of conflict of interest in that he had represented someone who had some prior contact with this case. Kirell felt this was the last straw and he announced to the court that he would be representing himself for the trial. Trial judges recognize the dangers of self-representation. However, the US Supreme Court has held that every defendant has an absolute right to be his own attorney.

The ***Faretta v.California*** case held that the Sixth Amendment had made applicable to the States by the Fourteenth Amendment guarantees that a defendant in a state criminal trial has an independent constitutional right of self-representation and that he may proceed to defend himself without counsel when he voluntarily and intelligently elects to do so.

However, the big question is what is considered an 'intelligent' election to represent oneself. Judges at first believed that they needed to question the defendant as to how well did he understand the criminal law and criminal procedure? Judges tried to find ways of testing defendants to see if they had the competence to try their case. Later appellate courts criticized those judges who discouraged defendants from being their own attorney. The appellate courts made it almost mandatory that if someone wanted to represent themselves the trial court couldn't prevent it.

The old saying was that if someone represented themselves they have a fool for a client. In some cases judges have provided certain defendants with an advisory attorney who assists with the legal procedures but that attorney would not ask any questions or conduct any cross-examination. Kirell believed in his own competency and ability to use his street smarts to carry him through any situation. Since Kirell had grown up in the juvenile court system, he was familiar with the manner of questioning witnesses on the witness stand. He felt that he was exceptionally good at cross-examining witnesses.

Thus began the trial of Kirell Taylor represented by Kirell Taylor. At first it was easy for him since all he had to do was sit at counsel table and listen to prosecutor Shelly Samuels ask questions of the prosecution witnesses. When Lorie Rawlings testified to what she heard and did, Kirell didn't have any problem. The next witnesses were the officers who responded to the Rawlings' house as well as the officer who went in pursuit of the Bentley. It was one witness after another and Kirell did little in the way of cross-examining them.

Then the detectives testified to finding the various pieces of evidence at the crash scene. Kirell was quiet and polite as the detectives explained what they found. It was the finding of the ski mask that elicited the most questions from Kirell. He didn't dispute where the ski masks were found but he was most interested as to how the masks were picked up and stored as evidence.

The questioning of Detective Powell by the prosecution brought in incriminating evidence of finding the bracelet and earring in Kirell's bedroom. Kirell's main response and attack was on the fact that there were other such bracelets and earrings produced and sold to the public. There were no serial numbers on the jewelry that one could say absolutely that this was Lorie's jewelry.

Likewise the detective said he found the business card in a Koran (Islamic sacred book), Kirell asked if the cards were given out as one of a kind or had they been handed out to many potential customers.

It wasn't until the prosecutor started asking questions about the conversation that the detective had with Kirell that the defendant reacted by questioning the witness. The detective indicated that he received a phone call from Kirell as the police were about to conduct search warrants on Kirell's bedroom, his girlfriend's place, and the Mustang. In his cross-examination of Powell, Kirell continued to cross-examine why he, Kirell, was never told the real reason they were taking a blood sample from him. Kirell wanted to dwell on the point that he never gave them consent to have a nurse draw his blood.

The prosecution had called all their witnesses except for the DNA expert. The jury was aware that detective Powell had sent the ski masks to SID to see if they could obtain cellular material from around the mouth area. After samples were obtained they were sent to the CellMark lab for analysis. The prosecution called the DNA expert who testified that CellMark lab analyzed the material found around the ski masks. They also analyzed the blood sample with the defendant's name on it.

The DNA expert testified that the match was 1 to 400,000. This was the most incriminating evidence against Kirell. The prosecutor was pleased that all the evidence had come in as the DNA connecting Kirell Taylor to the crashed Bentley.

CHAPTER 16 - KIRELL AND DNA EXPERT

The prosecution had completed the questioning of the DNA expert. It was time for Kirell to conduct his cross-examination of the prosecution's DNA expert.

Everyone in the courtroom had to be wondering how was a person like Kirell Taylor going to question a scientist on the details of the DNA analysis. Kirell was a person who lacked any formal education and had limited reading skills so how would he be able to discuss scientific points with such an expert.

However, Kirell had a game plan as to how he was going to use the prosecution DNA expert to show that the crime lab didn't do a complete examination of the materials from the ski masks. In order to create this doubt he asked the following questions:

Kirell Q. YOU NEVER KNEW EXACTLY THAT THE GENETIC ALLELES THAT YOU WERE TESTING WERE AMYLASE ENZYME?

Expert A. OKAY. AMYLASE, THE ENZYME, IS A PROTEIN AND D.N.A. IS A NUCLEIC ACID. THEY'RE VERY DIFFERENT. THE TESTS THAT I DO, EVEN THOUGH PROTEINS ARE PRESENT, IT ESSENTIALLY IGNORES THEM.

Kirell Q. SO IN YOUR OPINION, YOU WERE NOT SURPRISED THAT AMYLASE WOULD BE AROUND THE MOUTH AREA, CORRECT?

Expert A. THAT'S TRUE, YES, I WASN'T SURPRISED AT ALL.

Kirell Q. BUT YOU DID FAIL TO CONDUCT AN AMYLASE ENZYME MAPPING TEST, CORRECT?

The jurors had to be impressed that here was a gangster type asking sophisticated questions about the proper way to test for DNA. Kirell tried to set up the DNA expert by claiming another expert used a more thorough method. Kirell did it by asking the following:

Kirell Q. HOW LONG HAVE YOU BEEN PERFORMING CYTOLOGY TESTING?

Expert A. CYTOLOGY? IF YOU MEAN SEROLOGY, I'VE BEEN DOING IT FOR NEARLY 10 YEARS.

Kirell Q. DO YOU KNOW MARC TAYLOR PERSONALLY?

Expert A. YES, I DO.

Kirell Q. HE'S VERY WIDE KNOWN D.N.A. EXPERT THROUGHOUT THE SCIENTIFIC COMMUNITY.

Expert A. I GUESS YOU COULD SAY THAT.

Kirell tried to show that another DNA expert used a different protocol when conducting his DNA testing. This other method was called 'amylase mapping.' Some of the jurors may have been stunned that Kirell was capable of having a dialogue about the subject. At the end of the discussion the DNA expert explained why he didn't use the protocol by saying,

Expert A. LET'S PUT IT THIS WAY, IT'S A VERY CREATIVE PROTOCOL AND IT MAY VERY WELL BE SOUND, BUT I DON'T KNOW OF ANY OTHER LABORATORY THAT EMPLOYS THAT PARTICULAR PROTOCOL."

Kirell kept coming up with more questions about why LAPD crime lab didn't do "AP mapping' The DNA expert was trying to explain that it was a test but it had nothing to do with obtaining a DNA reading.

Kirell Q. SO HYPOTHETICALLY SPEAKING, IF THE WINDSHIELD HAD A PUNCTURE HOLE IN IT AND WATER SEEPED IN OR, BETTER YET, HYPOTHETICALLY SPEAKING, IF YOU WERE GIVEN INFORMATION THE MASK MAY HAVE BEEN WET, HYPOTHETICALLY SPEAKING, IF YOU WERE GIVEN INFORMATION THAT MASK MAY HAVE BEEN WET WOULD YOU HAVE CONDUCTED A CHARACTERIZATION TEST AROUND THE MOUTH AREA?

Expert A. NO. I'VE BEEN DOING THIS FOR 10 YEARS AND I'VE NEVER EVEN DONE AN A.P. MAPPING TEST. I'VE NEVER HAD A NEED TO.

Kirell Q. BUT AN A.P. MAPPING TEST CAN TELL YOU IF HIGH CONCENTRATION OF AMYLASE ENZYNE IS DETECTED, CORRECT?

Expert A. I MEAN THERE'S TESTS THAT CAN TELL ME THE CHEMICAL COMPOSITION OF THE DYE USED IN THE YARN, BUT I'M NOT INTERESTED IN THAT. MY FOCUS IS ON CELLULAR MATERIAL PRESENT; YES OR NO THE ANSWER WAS YES.

Kirell seemed to be able to come up with terms he could use in asking questions of the DNA expert. However he seemed to get tripped up asking the following questions.

Kirell Q. AND DOES THE SPERM CELL DIFFERENTIATE BETWEEN A MUCUS CELL OR A SWEAT?

At that point the DNA expert said

Expert A. THE USE OF THE WORD DIFFERENTIATE. I DON'T KNOW WHERE YOU ARE GOING WITH THAT?

KirelL Q. YOUR HONOR I HAVE NO FURTHER QUESTIONS FOR THIS WITNESS. HE'S BEING ELUSIVE

It seemed like the show was over and Kirell had shown that he could handle himself. And his 15 minutes of fame was about over as he asked one too many questions.

Kirell Q. YOU FAILED TO CONDUCT A CHARACTERIZATION OF THE SALIVA, CORRECT?

Expert A. I DIDN'T FAIL TO DO ANYTHING. I WAS COMPLETELY WITHIN OUR PROTOCOL AND THE PROTOCOL THAT LAPD USES WHICH IS APPROVED BY THE AMERICAN SOCIETY OF CRIME LAB DIRECTORS, DNA ADVISORY BOARD, MANY OTHER AGENCIES, THEY DON'T CALL FOR AP MAPPING. IT'S NOT ESSENTIAL TO MY GOAL, WHICH WAS DNA TYPING.

This ended one of the most remarkable courtroom moments when a Pacoima Piru Blood gangster tried to play the role of a high-powered Defense attorney. He had a few moments when all his practicing seemed to pay off. The question was how captivated were the jurors? Did he generate any sympathy for his plight? Did he create a reasonable doubt as to the conclusion that it was Kirell's DNA on the ski mask?

CHAPTER 17- KIRELL TAKES WITNESS STAND

The cross-examination by Kirell piqued the interest of the jurors as to what would be the Defense in the case. The judge asked the Defense attorney, Mr. Kirell Taylor, who he wished to call as his next witness. He uttered the name **KIRELL TAYLOR**. The judge said, Okay Mr. Taylor you may walk over to the witness stand.

A smirk flashed over Kirell's face as though he was about to enjoy the time of his life. Kirell turned and walked behind the prosecutor and his expression turned stern as he stepped to the witness chair and stopped. The courtroom clerk asked him to raise his right hand and she said, "You do solemnly swear that the testimony you may give in the case now pending before this court shall be the truth, the whole truth, and nothing but the truth, so help you God."

The jurors listened intently to hear Kirell say "I do." But did Kirell honestly plan to tell the truth and nothing but the truth? How was the questioning of this witness going to take place? Was Kirell going to ask himself a question and then give an answer to that question? This whole procedure of a pro per defendant testifying is a very awkward and surreal experience.

All of a sudden Kirell found himself seated in the witness chair and looked around the courtroom with the self-conscious expression saying, 'Okay what happens next?' There was a dull silence as the judge, prosecutor, courtroom clerk, court reporter and bailiff didn't say one word as to what he was to say or do. Kirell turned his head in the direction of the jury and could see the 12 of them and the two alternate jurors staring directly at him.

Kirell had found himself in difficult situations before and somehow he was always able to find words to say. This time was no exception as he addressed the jurors and said the following: (This is from a transcript of his testimony which contains his wording and some misspelling.)

LADIES AND GENTLEMEN OF THE JURY, I REALLY DON'T HAVE A CLUE AS TO WHAT I'M SUPPOSED TO SAY HERE ON THE STAND, SO I'M JUST GOING TO SPEAK MY PEACE.

BUT MY DEFENSE ABSOLUTELY REVOLVES AROUND ME BEING FRAMED BY THE LOS ANGELES POLICE DEPARTMENT BACK IN 1999 OF JULY AND THROUGHOUT THIS PHASE OF MY LIFE IN DEALING WITH THIS SYSTEM, I'VE REALLY BEGUN TO SEE THE INJUSTICES, THE GAMES, SUCH AS JUST NOW STATE YOUR NAME FOR THE RECORD. EVERYBODY KNOWS MY NAME. I'M SELF REPRESENT MYSELF. SO IT'S A LOT OF GAMES AND PLOYS AND TRICKS THAT'S PLAYED WITHIN THIS WHOLE TRIAL.

MY WHOLE LIFE HAS BEEN TURNED UPSIDE DOWN, NOT THAT ANYONE CARES. I'M NOT HERE FOR THE JURY'S SYMPATHY, NONE OF THAT. I WANT YOU TO TAKE HEED TO THE FACTS OF THE CASE AS THEY'RE PRESENTED TO YOU.

LIKE I SAY YOU KNOW, I'M NOT AN ATTORNEY, BUT I DO KNOW HOW TO READ TODAY. WHEN I WAS 17 YEARS OLD, I DIDN'T KNOW HOW TO READ. I LEARNED HOW TO READ WHILE I WAS IN PRISON AND GOING THROUGH JUVENILE HALL AUTODIDACTICALLY SELF-TAUGHT. I HAVE A VERY EXTENSIVE VOCABULARY.

I CONSIDER MYSELF TO BE A VERY WISE MAN, BUT NONETHELESS, THROW THAT ASIDE, I WANT TO GIVE IT TO YOU THIS CASE. THESE FACTS, MY TESTIMONY, THE WAY IN WHICH WE ALL CAN COMMUNICATE BECAUSE IT WILL BE STUPID UPON ME TO SIT UP AND TALK BY SIX SYLLABLE WORDS WHEN I MAY NOT KNOW WHO IS GRASPING THE MEANING OF THEM.

How much of his testimony was having a positive effect on the jury may be questionable? He had just told the jurors that he didn't want to use six syllable words since they weren't capable of grasping the meaning of those words.

Then Kirell wanted to explain to the jury how LAPD had been deceptive with him. He went on and on saying that they never told him why they were investigating him. Some jurors had a puzzled look on their faces as to why he was so fixated on the fact that LAPD didn't reveal to him the reason for the investigation. For over 15 minutes he continued to try to explain that the detectives weren't being candid with him. Kirell went on to tell the jury the following:

NEVERTHELESS, THEY NEVER TELL ME WHY I'M GOING TO JAIL. SO I HAD TO TAKE A STANCE AND TELL THIS GENTLEMAN RIGHT HERE.

AND YOU GUYS HAVE PROBABLY SEEN TODAY I CAN BECOME A LITTLE IRATE. I CAN BECOME UPSET. WE'RE ALL HUMAN. EVERYBODY OUT THERE HAS A NAVEL. IF NO ONE ON THAT PANEL HAS NOT GOT A NAVEL, STAND UP.

It seemed strange to be talking about 'jurors' navels' in a courtroom. Kirell wanted the jurors to understand why he was so upset about not knowing why he was being investigated. He went on to say:

AT THIS TIME IN MY LIFE, MY GOAL WAS TO GET OFF PAROLE. MY GOAL IS TO CHECK INTO THE UNITED STATES ARMS FORCES. SO I'M NOT A COWARD, ESPECIALLY TO GO ENTER AND WORK FOR THE UNITED STATES ARMY.

Those who had served in the armed forces may not have been overly impressed that Kirell felted he would have fit in well in the Army. Then Kirell went on to say that he understood the Hawthorne residential robbery but not the Rawlings robbery/murder. He went on to tell the jury the following:

THEY NEVER TELL ME. SO FINALLY DETECTIVE MENA (Hawthorne detective) TELLS ME, WELL, YOU ARE GOING TO JAIL FOR A ROBBERY IN HAWTHORNE AND THEY BRINGS AND SHOWS ME A PHOTO OF HER SUSPECT THAT DID THIS ROBBERY CHARGE.

I KNEW HIM. HIS NAME'S ERIC STERLING. I MET ERIC STERLING ONE TIME.AND THE TIME THAT I MET ERIC STERLING WAS ON MAY11TH. I DID A SHOW AT A CLUB CALLED BARBARY COAST IN GARDENA, CALIFORNIA. IT'S A STRIP CLUB AND I WENT AND DID A RAP SHOW THERE AND AFTER THAT WE ALL LEFT AND WE CARPOOLED TO NORM'S RESTAURANT OFF OF CENTURY.

Kirell's explanation was that his personal items such as wallet and ID were in the trunk of the car that was involved in the Hawthorne robbery. For some reason he wanted the jury to understand that he didn't care about the Hawthorne robbery since he had nothing to do with it. He goes on testifying as follows:

SO ONCE SHE SHOWS ME THE PHOTO, I KNOW WHO HE IS, INSIDE THE PAROLE UNIT. SHE TAKES ME AND TELLS ME, "I'M BOOKING YOU FOR THE ROBBERY IN HAWTHORNE."

NOW THEY ASK ME WOULD I BE WILLING TO GIVE UP YOUR BLOOD AND SALVIA. AND I SAID YES.

SO AT THIS TIME I'M THINKING EVERYONE IN THE UNIT IS FROM HAWTHORNE DIVISION. SO WE COME DOWN HERE TO VAN NUYS JAIL. SHE WAITS OUTSIDE OF THE LAB.

SO I'M RAP SINGING BECAUSE I TELL THEM "WHERE IS MY PAROLE AGENT?" IF ALL THIS NEED TO BE DONE, WHY IS SHE LEAVING ME, WHY WASN'T SHE HERE?

NO ONE IS TELLING ME ANYTHING AGAIN. THEY NOW, YOU HAVE TO MIND YOU, THESE CORRUPT COPS KNOW WHAT THEY DOING BELIEVE THAT

This line of testimony doesn't seem to be helping Kirell. He seemed fixated on the fact that LAPD obtained the blood from him by deceit. He went on to say:

WHAT'S UP WITH MY SALVIA, WHAT'S UP WITH MY BLOOD, WHAT'S UP WITH MY DNA?

..ANYWAY, I ASKED, "WHAT'S GOING ON WITH MY DNA MATERIAL?"

YOU SEE, THE TRICKERY AND THE GAME, IT'S LIKE YOU ALL LIKE OVER THERE SUSTAINED. WHAT DOES THAT MEAN? THAT MEAN I CAN'T KEEP ELABORATING, I CAN'T KEEP TALKING ABOUT IT, IT'S A BIG GAME, AND MY WHOLE LIFE IS ON THE LINE.

Kirell was representing himself and apparently, he didn't know that law enforcement can obtain bodily fluids for one case but still could use it in another case. Unfortunately, Kirell didn't see that he was painting a picture of being involved in the Rawlings robbery/murder. He didn't object to his DNA being used in a case where he knew that he was NOT involved. So why would he object to his blood being used in the Rawlings robbery/murder if he had nothing to do with that case. Or, did he have something to do with that case and he didn't want his DNA to be used against him?

CHAPTER 18- KIRELL DISLIKED THE DETECTIVES

Then Kirell wanted to discuss with the jury his disagreement with how the LAPD detectives conducted their interrogation of him.

I GET A VISITATION FROM POWELL AND WESTON IN THE JAIL SHOWING ME PHOTOS OF A BENTLEY AND ASKING ME DID I DRIVE THIS CAR AND GIVING ME A RUNDOWN ABOUT MR. CHRISTOPHER RAWLINGS. I TOLD HIM, YEAH, I SEEN THE INCIDENT ON THE NEWS. WHO DID IT? IT RAN ON THE NEWS FOR TWO WEEKS.

SO HE SAID, "DID YOU DRIVE THIS CAR?"

I TOLD HIM, "NO, I DIDN'T DRIVE THIS CAR." I TOLD HIM, "I WASN'T NEVER IN THIS CAR."

THEN HE TELLS ME MY BLOOD AT THE TIME, SO HE SAID, WAS RECOVERED ON THE SKI MASK. ALTOGETHER CLICKED IN AND I WENT BERSERK AND THEY TERMINATE THE INTERVIEW.

THEY WANTED TO TAKE MY FINGERPRINTS. I'M LIKE—YOU ALL SHOULD KNOW BY THEN—TAKE MY FINGERPRINTS? YOU KNOW, YOU ALREADY PLANTED THE DNA EVIDENCE FROM A CRIME I HAD NO KNOWLEDGE OF, AIN'T NEVER EVEN ATTENDED IN, AND NOW YOU WANT MY FINGERPRINTS IT'S NOT GOING TO HAPPEN.

BUT, AS YOU SEE HOW THIS JUDICIAL SYSTEM IS, THEY ORDERED IT ANYWAY. GOT MY PRINTS. LUCKILY THEY DIDN'T HAVE THE WILLPOWER OR INGENUITY, CREATIVITY ON HOW TO PLANT FINGERPRINTS.

Kirell wanted the jurors to understand all the disappointment he suffered since he couldn't find an attorney who was well versed in DNA. He explained to the jury he wanted to learn about DNA so he acted up in order to be sent to the hole (isolation part of jail) where it was quiet and he could read up on DNA. He called himself a "holebaby" which gave him the time to become an expert on DNA.

Then Kirell wanted to tell the jurors who in fact were the perpetrators of the Rawlings robbery/murder.

PUT IT THIS WAY: I KNOW WHO COMMITTED THIS CRIME, BOTH PERPETRATORS, AND CAN'T SPEAK ON IT, AS BAD AS IT'S KILLING ME EVERY DAY INSIDE, WHILE THEY SIT IN PRISON. BOTH GOT 15-YEAR SENTENCES.

This statement by Kirell was objected to and the judge told the jurors to disregard Kirell's statement. Then Kirell didn't know what else to say or do since he wanted to introduce hearsay statements that he claimed to have overheard on his jail tier. Kirell threw up his arms and told the jurors the following:

I GUESS I HAVE NOTHING FURTHER TO SAY AT THIS TIME IF I CAN'T—PUT IT THIS WAY: JUST JUDGE THE FACTS OF THE CASE.

IN FACT, I DON'T EVEN THINK IF WE ALL ARE BELIEVERS IN LIKE THEY SAY TELL THE TRUTH, THE WHOLE TRUTH AND NOTHING BUT THE TRUTH, SO HELP ME GOD. I DON'T BELIEVE NOBODY HAS A RIGHT TO JUDGE NOBODY. BUT THIS IS THE WAY THEY DESIGNED THIS SYSTEM FOR JUDGES, PEOPLE JUDGING AND POINTING THE FINGERS. LET GOD JUDGE YOU.

THAT'S THE WAY IT NEED TO BE IN IRAQ AND THE MIDDLE EAST. YOU DO A CRIME, YOU GET SENTENCED, YOU DID ON THE SPOT, PERIOD. BUT THEY GOT A SYSTEM OVER HERE WHERE THEY GOT JUDGES.

SO JUST JUDGE THE FACTS OF THE CASE. DON'T WORRY ABOUT SENDING ME TO PRISON IF THAT BE THE CASE. SEND ME. I'LL BE OUT REGARDLESS OF YOUR VERDICT LEGALLY BECAUSE I'M GOING TO STAY PURSUING MY FREEDOM.

JUDGE: MR. TAYLOR JUST STAY FOCUSED ON THE CASE,

DEFENDANT: I'M TRYING TO STAY FOCUSED ON THE CASE IN SO MANY WAYS AND LET THE JURY UNDERSTAND HOW IN WHICH I'VE LEARNED WHO COMMITTED THIS CRIME. AND YOU SUSTAINED THE OBJECTION.

JUDGE: YES

DEFENDANT: I DON'T HAVE NOTHING ELSE TO SAY. I CAN'T TELL YOU NOTHING. EVERYTHING I WANT TO TELL YOU, YOU ONLY GET FRAGMENTS, BITS AND PIECES.

It seemed that Kirell felt inhibited as to what he could tell the jury. Earlier he had told the jurors that a witness Ms. Reed (Pseudonym) had driven a long way from Pacoima to Hollywood to follow him home in south Los Angeles. This procedure seemed odd and the prosecutor tried to cross-examine him on the story he had told the jury. Was this witness to provide an alibi for Kirell? During this heated cross-examination Kirell wanted the jurors to hear that he was so concerned riding his motorcycle home on his own since it had been raining. The jurors had a perplexed look on their faces trying to decipher what Kirell was trying to say or imply.

The next area that Kirell was cross-examined on was the incriminating evidence in his bedroom. In particular how was he going to explain the finding in his bedroom of the bracelet, earring and the business card? Kirell was going to maintain that the items were planted by the detectives.

PROSECUTOR: HOW COULD YOU GET ONE OF YOUR LACKEYS TO DESTROY EVIDENCE IN YOUR HOUSE FROM THAT MURDER IF YOU DIDN'T KNOW YOU WERE A SUSPECT IN THAT MURDER?

KIRELL: IF I HAD KNOWLEDGE OF BEING INVOLVED IN A CRIME THAT DEALT WITH KILLING CHRISTOPHER RAWLINGS, FIRST OF ALL, I'M NOT GOING TO LEAVE INCRIMINATING EVIDENCE IN MY BEDROOM.

SECOND OF ALL, IF I HAD KNOWLEDGE OF BEING INVOLVED IN THIS CRIME, WHEN I BECAME ARRESTED OR WHENEVER IT COULD HAVE BEEN DESTROYED.

PROSECUTOR: YOU ARE SAYING IT WOULD HAVE BEEN BECAUSE YOU WOULD HAVE CALLED ONE OF THOSE PEOPLE WHO YOU HAVE LISTED AND ASKED THEM TO DESTROY THAT EVIDENCE, ISN'T THAT CORRECT?

KIRELL: IF I WOULD HAVE KNOWN—AND I KNEW YOUR MOTHER, I WOULD HAVE CALLED YOUR MOTHER AND DECEIVED HER TO TELL HER CAN YOU PLEASE GO PICK UP THESE ITEMS FROM SUCH AND SUCH LOCATION?

IF I HAD INCRIMINATING EVIDENCE IN MY BEDROOM I WOULD HAVE HAD A FRIEND DESTROY IT. ANYBODY WOULD HAVE GOTTEN RID OF ITEMS.

IF I HAD AN AFFECTION FOR GEORGE BUSH, GEORGE WILLIAMS BUSH, THE UNITED STATES PRESIDENT, IF I HAD AN AFFECTION FOR HIM, AS CRIMINALISTICS AS HE IS, HE WOULD HAVE DID IT FOR ME, TOO.

PROSECUTOR: YOU ARE TELLING US THAT ALL THESE PEOPLE, HAD YOU HAD INCRIMINATING EVIDENCE LINKING YOU TO THIS MURDER, ALL THESE PEOPLE WOULD HAVE BEEN MORE THAN WILLING TO COME IN AND DESTROY THAT EVIDENCE ON YOUR BEHALF, IS THAT CORRECT?

KIRELL: THAT'S ABSOLUTELY CORRECT.

His Defense might have been better if he just denied ever having the items. However, Kirell wanted the jurors to see how if he had the incriminating items that he could have had someone go into his bedroom and destroy them before the police could find them. He seemed to be proud that he could outsmart the cops.

After Kirell was finished testifying the evidence portion of the trial was over. Both sides were given an opportunity to argue their case. The Argument phase of a case was definitely advantageous for the pro per defendant. If the defendant does an outstanding job the jurors are going to be impressed. They may have a feeling that the guy has some potential so let's give him a break. On the hand if the defendant does a pathetic job representing himself, some jurors are going to be sympathetic and start rooting for the underdog.

Kirell's Argument was that of a bitter young man in which he wanted to attack the detectives. He never could come up with a plausible explanation for how the incriminating evidence got into his bedroom. His argument regarding his DNA on the ski mask was one of the areas where he lost his focus. All he wanted the jury to know was how deceptive the LAPD detectives were in obtaining his blood sample. He couldn't see that there were better arguments he could make such as chain of evidence or some type of error in the DNA testing.

The jury deliberated and came back GUILTY on the first-degree murder as well as all the other charges. At the time of sentencing, he received a sentence of Life in state prison without the possibility of parole. The old adage that the defendant who represents himself at trial has a fool for a client was never truer than in Kirell Taylor's case.

CHAPTER 19- WHO'S THE OTHER SUSPECT?

The LAPD detectives had to be elated that they had been successful in apprehending and convicting one of the robbers who killed Christopher Rawlings. Much intensive investigative work as well as a few tips led to the arrest of Kirell Taylor. However, bringing **BORIS GRAHAM** to Justice was going to take a great deal more gumshoe detective work and steely resolve.

In order to build a case on Boris Graham one needs to revisit the night of the incident. Remember that Kaiser Permanente Hospital received a call from Wilma Carson asking if they had a patient by the name of Boris Graham who was injured in a traffic accident. The next day the detectives had interviewed her and learned that she was Boris' girlfriend who had mothered their two children. She claimed that they didn't get along and she hadn't seen him for several days.

Nothing ever developed from the inquiry to the hospital about a Boris Graham. It wasn't until six months later on August 16, 1999, that the detectives received a call from Detective Gordon (Pseudonym) from the LAPD Foothill Division. Detective Gordon indicated that he had received an anonymous call from a female who said that she knew who murdered the "Rich guy in the Bentley." Since the Foothill Division wasn't conducting the investigation of that case, he really wanted her to talk to the detectives at West Valley Division.

However, this Foothill detective tried to elicit as much information from the caller as he could because anonymous callers will give up if they feel they are merely being transferred to someone else (called the bureaucratic merry-go-round). He tried to obtain more information from her, however, he realized that anonymous callers don't want to give out too much information that might reveal their identity. Eventually she was willing to provide the name of the robber as a Boris Graham but she didn't want to say how she knew him. When asked where he lived, she didn't give an address but merely said he lived with his brother Robert Graham (Pseudonym) in Canoga Park.

The Foothill Division detective didn't know if this was important information or simply some female who was trying to burn an old boyfriend. He called the West Valley Division detectives and said he received info about a Boris Graham from an anonymous caller. He was somewhat apologetic since it wasn't very explicit as to details.

The Rawlings detectives said that this was a form of déjà vu since they remembered the name being mentioned by a caller to Kaiser Hospital asking about an injured Boris Graham. The detectives said that they appreciated the info and would make another note in the file about the anonymous call.

Often cases are solved by mere flukes that just happen. The following set of events is highly convoluted. It is the beginning of a road that takes a number of twists and turns. Eventually the road leads directly to Boris Graham.

On August 19.1999, a few days after that anonymous call two LAPD officers were on patrol when they noticed a speeding Honda going north on Sherman Way. The officer got behind the Honda and turned on the lights and siren and within a block the car pulled to the curb. There were two young male blacks in the car. The officer who was driving approached the driver and asked for his driver's license. The driver slowly reached for his wallet and took out his driver's license with the name Robert Graham.

The other officer asked the passenger for some form of identification and he produced an Illinois driver's license in the name of Kato Austin. The officer looked at the license and asked him where he lived and he explained that he now lived in Chicago and was merely visiting Los Angeles. The one officer collected the two licenses and walked back to the patrol unit to run the names through the computer.

The DMV computer database was slow in responding. As the officer in the police car was waiting for the information the dispatcher came over the radio exclaiming that there was a robbery with a gun, just off of Sherman Way. The dispatcher wanted any units in the area to respond to the robbery.

The officer in the car leaned out and yelled to his partner that they needed to go on a hot call. The other officer hurriedly came back to the police car and the two officers sped off north on Sherman Way. By the time they reached the robbery site there were police units converging from all sides. Within minutes it was determined that the so-called robbery was a homeless man holding a subway sandwich in his hand. The two officers had to chuckle to themselves that maybe this was too much of an over-response.

Then their police car received another radio call and off they went in another direction. It wasn't until later that they noticed on the clipboard they still had the driver's licenses of Robert Graham and Kato Austin. The thought was how to return the licenses to the two parties. When they returned to the station, they ran both names looking for an address. What caught their attention was that Robert Graham was on parole. When they contacted his parole officer, she stated that Robert was in violation of parole and if they had further contact with him, he should be arrested for a violation of 3056 Penal Code. They further learned that there had been several recent robberies in which Robert fit the description and the vehicle was a Honda similar to the one Robert was driving.

The parole agent indicated that his listed residence was 21035 Bryant Street Apartment #3. Six days later on August 25th the officers went to that address and found Robert to be there with Kato Austin the other person who had been in the car with Robert. In the apartment was also a small child but no other adult caring for the child. The officers placed Robert Graham under arrest for the parole violation.

Earlier they had run the name of Kato Austin and discovered he had only a misdemeanor warrant. Robert was placed under arrest, however, the officers had one of those practical dilemmas. They could arrest Kato Austin on the outstanding misdemeanor warrant. However, if they did, they would have a small child to take care of. Someone at the station would have to babysit the child until a relative could be found.

The officers weighed the options and they decided to leave Kato Austin at the apartment to take care of the child. (What the officers didn't realize was that the person who claimed to be Kato Austin was none other than BORIS GRAHAM. The officers at the time didn't know they had in their grasp the second suspect in the Rawlings robbery/murder case. Consequently, Boris Graham was able to be on the run for the next FOUR YEARS.)

The officers drove away with Robert Graham handcuffed in the backseat of their police unit and oblivious to the true identity of Kato Austin. Often police officers react to gut feelings as to whether something is wrong. The one officer said to the other that she had mixed feeling leaving the child in the possession of that person named Kato Austin. At the next intersection, the driver made a wide U-turn and returned to the apartment.

The one officer went back into Apartment #3 and discovered that the child and that person claiming to be Kato Austin were long gone. This all seemed peculiar to the officer since they had been gone for less than five minutes.

The officers returned to the West Valley Division Jail and booked Robert Graham for the parole violation. The Rawlings detectives had placed a note in the police files that they wanted to be contacted if anyone came in contact with GRAHAM. The detectives got the word that Robert Graham was in custody, so they went to the jail to talk to him. The detectives asked him if he knew the whereabouts of his brother Boris Graham.

Robert's response of course was that he hadn't seen his brother for a while and didn't have a clue where he could be. He also denied that Kato Austin was staying with him. The detectives again were coming up with giant goose egg.

The detectives were pleased with the progress of connecting Kirell Taylor to the Rawlings robbery/murder. As to the other suspect they didn't have any leads. They had the feeling that they were merely spinning their wheels and getting nowhere. Time moved on to the first of September when the one of the lead detectives on the Rawlings case walked by another detective who was trying to assemble a photo line-up of the Graham brothers. That detective had an Illinois driver's license of a Kato Austin also on his desk. That was when the Rawlings detective noticed that the photos of Boris Graham and Kato Austin were of the same person. The Rawlings detective took possession of the Kato Austin's Illinois driver's license.

When the Rawlings detective contacted the Illinois DMV about the Kato Austin driver's license, he learned that the address that was on the license didn't exist anywhere in Chicago.

It wasn't until September 14, 1999 that CLUE #22 came about. A desk officer from LAPD Foothill Division called the Rawlings detective and said that he had received a peculiar call from an anonymous male caller who asked if LAPD would extradite a person on a felony warrant. The desk officer told the caller that they could and the caller immediately terminated the conversation. Minutes later the caller called back and said, "I know who the driver was in the Christopher Rawlings murder." That surprised the desk officer and his reaction was to ask who that person was. The caller hesitated for a moment and replied that it was a Michael Parks **(His moniker was the name Chicken)** who was in custody in the Chicago Cook County jail.

When this information was revealed to the Rawlings detectives, they had mixed feelings as to this information. They had been down this road before about bogus information from anonymous callers. However, what aroused their curiosity was the fact that they had received information about a Kato Austin in Chicago.

One of the detectives grabbed the phone and called Chicago PD to ask them about a Michael Parks who was supposed to be in police custody. After being transferred around several times he was able to reach the officer knowledgeable about Michael Parks. The Chicago officer checked out the status of Michael Parks and stated that he was in custody on a narcotics case. When asked how long he would be in custody, the Chicago officer indicated that he was likely to be released.

Then the LAPD detectives contacted their boss who approved for them to fly to Chicago. The detectives caught a red-eye flight and were in Chicago the next morning. They arranged to meet Michael Parks at the Cook County Jail. They read him the Miranda Rights and he agreed to waive them and talk to the detectives. The detectives didn't know where this conversation was going since the anonymous caller had accused him as being one of the robbers in the Rawlings case.

Instead of a frontal assault on Mr. Parks the one detective pulled out photo line-ups one including Kirell's photo and the other showing Boris Graham's photos. Parks looked at them and without hesitation said that he recognized Kirell Taylor. When he looked at Boris Graham's photo, he nodded that he was a fellow Pacoima Piru Blood gang member.

The detectives didn't know what to think but they wanted to get a blood sample from Michael Parks. They also wanted a saliva sample and were in the process of obtaining it. Parks continued to look at the photo line-up with Boris' photo in it. Parks' face lit up with a smile and he took his index finger and waved it around pointing at Boris' photo and said "That's what this is about! That mother fucker Booney."

The detectives responded by asking if it had something to do with Boris Graham. Parks shook his head and said that was what he got from helping out little Booney who he said was really Boris. He explained that earlier in the year around June he got a call from Boris saying he and a friend, Shake, needed a place to stay and asked to stay with him in his mother's apartment.

Parks agreed that they could stay but it would be crowded since his girlfriend, Friday Hanson (Pseudonym), was staying with Parks. Boris and his friend showed up and moved right in. While they were staying with Parks there were many conversations among the group of them.

Boris said that he and Kirell had 'jacked' a white guy at this house in Los Angeles and had taken his Roll Royce (sic). They threw the rich guy into the trunk of the car and went into the rich guy's house but there was nothing there. He said that there was a police pursuit and they crashed the Rolls Royce. When the car crashed the victim was 'spit out the trunk' and killed. He said that Boris was mad at Kirell because on the night of the incident Kirell made a stupid mistake and called his sister and told her to call around to look for him. Because of that Boris believed that the police had gotten his name as a suspect in the murder. He went on to say that his sister called his girlfriend Wilma, who started making some calls to the area hospitals and jails looking for him. He told Parks that it was a Mexican guy, named Angel who set up the robbery. That guy moved to Sacramento area and Boris had given him a blue face Rolex watch. Later Boris wanted it back and was going to give Angel $200 for it

While Boris was staying with Parks, Boris indicated he wanted to obtain an Illinois driver's license in another name. Boris decided to use the name Kato Austin on the license since he knew such a person who lived in Los Angeles. One of the requirements for getting a driver's license in Illinois was that Boris had to have a car in order to take the driving test. Parks talked his mother into loaning her car to Boris so he could take the driving test.

Parks and his mother tried to be accommodating to their visitors from Los Angeles. Boris and his friend Shake totally took advantage of the situation. However, after several months these guys wore out their welcome. For one thing these guests ran up a huge phone bill and didn't offer to reimburse the Parkses. Eventually, it became so bad that Boris didn't show any respect for Parks' mother who was preparing the food and cleaning up after them.

Words were exchanged and eventually it became intolerable. Michael Parks told his old homies Boris and Shake that they were no longer welcomed. Begrudgingly Boris moved out but he left his displeasure by slashing the tires on Michael's mother's car. This whole incident left a bad taste in Michael's mouth.

He most likely wouldn't have said anything negative about his old homie Boris, if Boris hadn't been so unappreciative for all that Michael and his mother had done for him and Shake. Luckily the detectives had caught Michael Parks at the perfect time in which he was mad at Boris. As much as Michael disliked Boris, he wasn't motivated to be overly helpful to the LAPD detective.

Michael Parks after agreeing to waive his Miranda Rights and talk to the detectives made it abundantly clear that he would not talk if a tape recorder was used. Michael was no dummy. Even though Detective Powell indicated that someone had named him as one of the robbers, Michael wasn't that concerned since he had plenty of people who would provide him with an alibi. Michael could see that he had the upper hand in this discussion. Michael was 'street smart.' He wasn't going to give up his Ace cards without getting something in return.

He would only allow his statements to be taped if he was guaranteed some leniency or released on bail on the current narcotics charges in Chicago. He went so far as to refuse to sign any documents about the LA case.

Since Detective Powell was so eager to solve the Rawlings case, he immediately agreed to talk to the Cook County DA's Office to see if they could somehow give Michael some type of break on his narcotics case. Could they reduce the charges or even give him a reduced bail? Detective Powell soon learned how things are done in the windy city. One of the Cook County prosecutors told Detective Powell the facts of life. Their DA's Office made it clear that they wouldn't agree to any type of deal on a case 'outside their jurisdiction.' In other words, if Chicago wasn't getting something out of it then there is NO DEAL for Michael Parks.

Needless to say, Detective Powell was seriously disappointed that he wasn't going to get a tape-recorded statement from Michael Parks which spelled out Boris' involvement in the Rawlings case. However, Detective Powell wasn't the type to give up easily. He remembered Michael saying that his girlfriend, Friday Hanson was living with him while Boris was staying at his mother's house. Powell asked one of the Chicago detectives if he could track down where the girlfriend was presently living.

Moments later Detective Powell was given an address on the Southside of Chicago where Friday Hanson lived. Although the Cook County DA's Office hadn't been overly cooperative to Powell, the Chicago Police Department was more accommodating. They drove Powell out to Miss Hanson's place. Powell met with her and indicated that he was trying to help her boyfriend. He indicated that he was trying to learn more about the whereabouts of Boris Graham.

She admitted that Boris had lived with Michael and her for several months during the summer of 1999. Since Boris had been such a jerk, she didn't hesitate being frank about his behavior. Powell asked if he could tape record her conversation. She had no difficulty with that. He asked her what she remembered Boris talking about. She indicated that she knew him as Bonney who continually bragged about doing a robbery where a rich guy in LA was killed. Boris described that the rich guy had a safe that they were going to rob and some guy with a Spanish name supposedly set it up.

She recalled that Michael and Booney got into a big argument over the damage to Parks' car. As a result, Michael threw Boris and Shake out of the house. As far as she knew Booney moved to Las Vegas and Shake returned to Los Angeles.

Powell asked her if Boris had left anything behind when he moved out. She didn't think so but she told Powell he could look around especially in several boxes they had moved from Michael's mother's place. Powell found some letters and cards addressed to Boris Graham and even some items with the name Kato Austin on them.

When Detective Powell returned to Los Angeles, he checked on Shake and located his mother. She said that Shake was staying with his brother Amin on Sherman Way. Powell went to that address and located Shake's brother but not Shake. Amin admitted that he didn't like Boris and thought he was trouble and he wouldn't let him stay with them.

Amin didn't know the whereabouts of Boris but he remembered that he had a girlfriend who lived in Palmdale. He recalled that she had a name like Mugly but she was better known as Kim.

Detective Powell had to decompress from his long trip to Chicago. Originally, he flew to Chicago to check out an anonymous call to the police in which someone claimed that it was a Michael Parks who was the other suspect in the Rawlings case. When he checked out Michael Parks, he was convinced that Boris Graham was the true second suspect. After obtaining a taped statement from Michael's girlfriend, Powell was satisfied that he finally had enough evidence. On September 23, 1999, the DA's Office prepared a complaint and an arrest warrant for Boris Graham for the murder of Christopher Rawlings and all the additional charges.

CHAPTER 20- TAYLOR SPILLED THE BEANS

The television show, *America's Most Wanted*, aired the episode again on the Rawlings case. As a result new interest was generated for finding the other suspect. It wasn't until January 28, 2004 that time ran out for Boris Graham and he was arrested in Hollywood, Florida. He was extradited back to Los Angeles where his case was set for trial.

After Kirell Taylor was convicted in the Rawlings case and sentenced to state prison for life without parole, he had time to think about the unfairness that existed throughout the world. It didn't seem fair that Boris Graham his partner in crime still hadn't been convicted of the same charges as he had. In September of 2006, the lead Detective Powell received one of the most unusual letters. Throughout his long career as a detective he had never received a letter where one suspect wanted to clear the air and point the finger to the other suspect.

Because of the job as a homicide detective one can become jaded about mankind. Receiving such a letter from someone he had helped convict of murder, the detective was ready for the unexpected. No murderer does a good deed without wanting something in return. Here was Kirell Taylor inviting the detective and prosecutor to visit him in his new home in state prison.

On September 21, 2006, the detective and the prosecutor took the long trip to the prison where Kirell was housed. When they entered the prison interview room it was like an old-time school reunion. Five years earlier they were all seated together in a contentious trial. Nobody knew exactly the proper thing to say in greeting each other. Obviously, it would be inappropriate to say to Kirell how are you enjoying your new living quarters. Or have you made any new friends up here?

The detective wasn't going to fall into the Michael Parks situation where he got all the damning statements and then Parks wouldn't let the detective record his statements. Although it was an awkward situation, the detective push the record button before Kirell could say anything. In order not to scare Kirell and cause him to clam up the detective started off with a safe topic by asking Kirell how well he knew Boris Graham and if he knew him by his moniker 'Little Booney.' Kirell hesitated for a moment and took time to clear his throat. The visitors waited to see Kirell's reaction. Kirell stiffened himself in the worn-out prison chair and he gave the impression that he had something on his chest he wanted to say.

All of sudden he started talking and acknowledged that he grew up with Boris in the same Pacoima neighbor. They both became involved with the local Piru gang and became homies. Kirell willingly admitted he knew Michael Parks as well as Irma Bijoux. This was all interesting for the detective to learn and record the conversation on tape recording, but was it going to be of any evidentiary value in Boris' trial?

The detective was treading gently since he didn't know how much Kirell would be willing to reveal. Did Kirell comprehend what he was doing? The tape recorder was on the table in front of him and the red light was on indicating that it was recording everything he was saying. There could be repercussions for him in prison if he ratted on one of his gang members.

Then the moment of truth came when the detective asked about the facts of the Rawlings case. Kirell took a deep breath and all of a sudden like a logjam breaking up he started divulging every nitty-gritty detail. He stated that it was his ex-girlfriend Irma Bijoux who dropped him and Boris off near the Rawlings' house. She was driving a green Mustang with a tan top. He and Boris wanted to find a place to hide while waiting for Rawlings to drive up to his house in his Bentley.

He explained that he and Boris moved up to the side of the garage and found a place in a planter bed where they could stand behind a tree which hid them from view. Both men had guns. One was a revolver and the other was a Glock 9-millimeter semi-automatic. These weapons would be used to scare the victims into complying with their commands. They brought with them two rolls of duct tape. One was for tying up the husband and the other to be used to restrain the wife. As they unobtrusively waited, they placed one of the rolls of duct tape on the ground in the planter.

Kirell ripped off a piece of the duct tape and used it to attach the police scanner to his sweatshirt. He had brought along the police scanner in order to listen to the police calls so they would know if the police had been alerted to their robbery. In order to gain control of the husband the plan was to use a pair of handcuffs to restrain him as they went through the house looking for valuables.

Kirell made it clear that their plan was not only to rob the victim but to carjack his Bentley. Then he started laying out the specifics for the detective and prosecutor. He explained every step of the robbery and as to who did what. He related that after hiding by the side of the garage they saw the Bentley drive into the driveway and stop to wait for the garage door to fully open. They both pulled ski masks down over their faces. They had to adjust the ski masks so they could see out of the slots for the eyes.

Then the driver slowly drove into the garage. Both robbers leaned down and followed the car into the garage. They could hear the radio continue to blare. Then almost automatically the garage door started to close by rolling down. Both were positioned behind the trunk lid and with their guns drawn they moved over to the driver's side of the Bentley. When the driver, Christopher Rawlings, stepped out of the car they both surrounded him with their guns pointing at him. Christopher had a surprised look on his face as though he couldn't comprehend what was happening.

They yelled at him in a loud rough voice to put his hands in front of him. One of the robbers suddenly placed handcuffs on his hands. However, Christopher seemed dazed and not knowing how to respond to the robbers. In order to impress the victim that they meant business they struck him several times in the face causing him to fall down on the hard concrete floor of the garage. The robbers kept shouting at him to get up and show them where the safe and valuables were located. After several tense moments Christopher rose up seeming dazed.

They continued to threaten him in hopes he would be more cooperative in showing them the location of the valuables. After several minutes Christopher stumbled his way over to the door to the laundry room. The two robbers followed directly behind him with their guns poking him in the back. They entered the house and directed him to take them to the master bedroom.

As they walked through the kitchen, they glanced around for the wife hoping to use the duct tape they were carrying to tie her up. One of them made a cursory sweep of the first floor but didn't find anyone. As Christopher led them to the stairs the other robber motioned with the gun to go upstairs. When they got to the top of the stairs Christopher tried to use his two handcuffed hands to point to the master bedroom.

Kitchen

Living Room Showing Stairs

All three of them moved into the main bedroom and the robbers continued to turn their ski masked heads back and forth as they were looking for something in particular. One of the robbers in exasperation asked, "Where's the safe." Christopher looked at him with a disbelief expression and said, "What?" The robber repeated, "You're safe!" At that point Christopher started to shake his head back and forth. He must have wondered whether the robbers were in the wrong house since he had no safe at his house.

As they entered the master bedroom one of the robbers scurried into the closet and groped around on the floor hoping to find a trap door to the safe. That robber exited the closet with a disappointed look on his face. Where could the safe be that they had been told about? As one robber continued to point the gun at Christopher the other walked over to the dresser. He took his gun and stuck it in his waistband so he had both hands free. On top of the dresser was a wooden jewelry box in which Lorie kept some of her Cartier jewelry. He quickly pulled open the little drawers and dumped the contents in the palm of his other hand.

Dresser in Master Bed Room

He was able to fill up his hand with bracelets, rings and earrings. After emptying the jewel box, he reached over to a blue-faced Rolex and picked it up with his other hand. By that time the robber started to place the items into his pants pockets. As they were milling around the master bedroom sounds came over the scanner indicating some type of police activity. It wasn't clear what the police dispatcher was saying but the two robbers nodded to each other that maybe it was time for them to go.

One of the robbers pushed Christopher toward the bedroom door. Christopher didn't resist but immediately walked out of the door and headed for the stairs. One of the robbers said to wait as he poked his head into every bedroom to see if there was anything easy to take. After looking into all the rooms, he motioned to the other robber to proceed downstairs with their hostage. Boris got behind Christopher and ordered him to return to the garage.

Kirell followed them to the kitchen where he stopped to look around for valuables. He saw a purse on one of the dining room chairs and walked over to it. He grabbed the purse and opened it. He turned it upside down and dumped the contents on the table. All sorts of papers and cards and a woman's makeup bag came falling out onto the little table. Finally, there was a thud as a large wallet fell out. He immediately snatched the wallet and started to leave the kitchen.

As Kirell went by the refrigerator he automatically opened the fridge door to see what was inside. With his ski mask on it was hard looking through the eye holes to see what goodies were inside. He could see a half-full carton of milk which he pushed to the side. He was hoping for a Colt 45 malt but he didn't expect to find one in a fridge in Woodland Hills. However, what caught his eye was a one-gallon container of orange juice that looked so cold and inviting. He couldn't resist the temptation and reached in with his glove-covered hand and pulled the orange juice out.

His mother had told him while growing up that it wasn't polite to drink from the container. Yet, under the circumstances he felt justified in tipping the container up in the air and drinking from it. The juice was so cold and it tasted so refreshing. He wanted to savor the moment but snapped back to reality and took one more swallow and placed the container down on the kitchen counter. He walked briskly over to the laundry door to re-enter the garage.

As he stepped into the garage, he saw Boris standing over Christopher who was on his hands and knees. Boris was rigidly holding his revolver against the victim's head. Kirell hadn't heard what Boris had said but he heard Christopher let out a bloody scream. Kirell's only thought was to finish up the robbery and get out of there in the Bentley. He grabbed Boris' gun and pushed it aside. Then he asked him what he was doing. By this time he had defused the situation and started methodically going through Christopher's pockets looking for valuables.

Out of one pocket Kirell pulled a money clip with $1,000 in cash and from the other pants pocket he got a wallet. Since Christopher was wearing a Rolex watch on one wrist, Kirell pulled it off and slipped it on his wrist. He glanced down at it and had a feeling of being a successful gangster. His old fellow gang buddies would be envious of him wearing a precious Presidential series Rolex. On Christopher's other wrist he noticed some type of gold bracelet. Kirell couldn't tell how valuable it was but he figured it was worth something if this guy wore a Rolex and drove a Bentley. With one forceful yank the bracelet flew off and he had it in his hand.

They could hear over the scanner the police dispatcher mentioning that the units were arriving at the Rawlingses' house on Quedo Drive. The two robbers looked at each other in wonderment. How did the cops know about the robbery? They hadn't seen or found the wife in the house so who could have tipped off the police? The two robbers' immediate attention was on how they were going to get away without being stopped by the police.

They fathomed that they couldn't drive out with the victim inside the car. On the other hand, they could leave him in the garage but they couldn't permit that since he would run out of the garage as soon as they opened the garage door. Boris came up from behind Christopher and grabbed him and unceremoniously threw him in the trunk. That solved their immediate problem and now how were they going to pull off the escape. They knew that when they backed out the Bentley from the closed garage, they were going to have company from the converging police cars.

Kirell decided to take the leadership role by climbing into the driver's seat and starting up the Bentley. Boris ran around to the other side and jumped in and slammed the passenger door. Both robbers had never driven a Bentley so they were staring at the dashboard trying to find the handle to place the car in reverse. When they felt they were in control of the Bentley, Kirell reached up on the visor for the remote control for the garage door. When his hand felt the controls, he pushed the button.

A slow grinding sound could be heard as the garage door rolled up. Kirell in the driver's seat turned his head to look to the rear. He couldn't see anyone and no police cars in view. He pressed down on the accelerator and the Bentley went into slow motion rolling out and down the driveway. Kirell hadn't spent the time to readjust the seat and he was having difficulty reaching the brake pedal. His foot continued to move from side to side attempting to find the brake. The Bentley continued to roll down the driveway and out into the street. The car came to an abrupt halt when the back tires struck the curb on the other side of the street.

That jolted both the robbers in their seats. They quickly glanced down the street to see if the coast was clear. When they looked to the left, they could see a police unit at the end of the street. Kirell felt a moment of panic but reacted by jerking the steering wheel to the right. He moved the shifter to 'Drive' and pressed as hard as he could on the accelerator. The Bentley has a reputation for being a smooth comfortable automobile but not known for jackrabbit starts. The Bentley Company prides itself for having a large powerful engine that slowly can propel the Bentley to high speed.

Kirell didn't want to attract attention but when he glanced at the rearview mirror, he could see flashing red lights. He turned up this two-lane residential street and didn't take his foot off the accelerator. As he approached Ventura Boulevard, he could see that the street he was on came to an end. That meant he would have to turn one way or the other. He decided to turn right in full throttle mode. The Bentley spun slightly to the right as the wheels skidded sideways letting out a squeal that could be heard for blocks. The robbers had to be captivated as to how well the Bentley performed at high speeds.

Since it was 9:00 p.m. the traffic on Ventura Boulevard was starting to thin out except for those who had been out doing some late shopping. Kirell was surprised that the police unit was able to follow the Bentley. By now the police car's siren was whaling. As Kirell and the Bentley roared east on Ventura Boulevard the speedometer reached 100 mph. Even under these extreme speeds the Bentley performed like a luxurious car.

As he approached Winnetka Avenue, Kirell could see through the rear-view mirror that the police car was now gaining on them. He could see that he was going to have to make a life-and-death decision. The signal at Winnetka was red and there was cross traffic. He knew if he stopped for the signal the cops would be able to catch him. He could take the old adage of 'damn the torpedoes full speed ahead' (This saying came from the Civil War, the Battle of Mobile, that Admiral Farragut shout this as he sailed his ship through a minefield)

Kirell thought there must be another way. He slowed the Bentley slightly so he could look for any cross traffic. When he could see it was all clear in the intersection, he gunned the engine and the Bentley accelerated through the red signal.

When he cleared that intersection, he gave it full throttle and started darting from one lane to the other lane as he passed traffic in front of him. By then he had the Bentley flying over 100 mph and seemed to have pulled away from the police unit. As he approached Tampa Avenue he thought if he turned north, the police might not notice that he had turned off of Ventura Boulevard.

He made a hard left turn and the Bentley slid sideways but he was able to keep the car on the road. Just as he negotiated the turn, he felt that he had ditched the cops. But as he sped north on Tampa Avenue, he came face to face with another police unit proceeding southbound. This surprised Kirell just as much as he surprised the two police officers in this different car. That unit had received a radio call to assist in a pursuit on Ventura Boulevard. When the officers saw the Bentley roar past them, they immediately made a U-turn to take up the pursuit.

Kirell saw a small blue Chevrolet pull out from a side street onto Tampa Avenue in the right lane. Kirell tried to move over into the left lane but a slow moving car was blocking him. Through the rearview mirror he could see the other police car make the U-turn and flip on its red lights and siren. He had to make a split-second decision whether to dash around the slow-moving car and pull back into the fast lane before hitting the Chevrolet. As he made the tricky maneuver, he started to pass the slow vehicle to his left side. At the same time, he could see the small blue Chevrolet directly in front of them.

All of a sudden, he noticed how slowly the Chevy was traveling. He could jam on the brakes to avoid a crash but at that instant he glanced in the mirror and saw the police unit appear to be gaining on them. His fear of the cops overran his judgment to hit the brakes. His foot hit the gas pedal and the Bentley jerked forward. As they flew down the slow lane all Kirell could see was the rear of the blue Chevrolet growing larger in front of him.

Then all of sudden he turned the steering wheel slightly to the left to move into the fast lane. In doing that the Bentley tapped the Chevrolet on the left rear bumper. It seemed like an innocent bump that could be described as a slight fender bender. To Kirell's surprise the small Chevrolet started rotating to the right as the Bentley acted like an expensive bulldozer slicing into the Chevrolet crushing the rear portion like stomping on a beer can.

The collision presented Kirell with some real challenges. Since he had never driven a Bentley, he had no idea how he should react to the collision. Should he brake or should he turn the steering wheel? He didn't need to make any decision since everything had been set in motion. At this time, he was being controlled by outside forces and he was merely on the ride of his life.

All he could see before his eyes was the Bentley starting to spin clockwise. The steering wheel was turning on its own. His hands were incapable of controlling the spinning of the steering wheel. He could hear the Chevrolet striking a street light pole making a loud screeching noise.

The Bentley continued at a high rate of speed like a rocket fired into space. All a sudden the front of the Bentley struck a high-voltage power pole and snapped it like a wooden matchstick. That jolted both Kirell and Boris like a pilot breaking the sound barrier. Instantaneously the airbags ignited and forced both of them back against the front seats. Then they felt the Bentley spin around like the teacup ride at Disneyland. They didn't know when or where they would come to rest. It was the branches of a giant sycamore tree that brought the Bentley to rest against its trunk.

The noise of the crash was deafening and caused the occupants to be disoriented. The two robbers had been in tough scrapes before but nothing like this. Now they were sandwiched by the airbags in a mangled Bentley that was totally black. Their senses were in overload but they noticed the faint smell of gasoline. Soon the darkness was broken by flickering flames coming from the engine compartment.

Although the two robbers wanted to escape the police, there was an initial interest in merely surviving this violent crash. Kirell waited for the airbag to deflate so he could assess the situation. Remarkably he was able to move his arms. Yet he had difficulty standing up on his wobbling legs. He looked over to Boris and could see that he had a pained look on his face. He was pinned against the seat by the inflated airbag. As the bag started shrinking, he could see his crime partner wincing in pain. The wailing of the police sirens from the arriving police cars was so loud he was unable to talk to Boris.

Kirell didn't want to leave Boris inside the Bentley for the police to capture. By this time, he was able to push the driver's door open sufficiently to climb out. As he stepped out, he turned to see if Boris was following. However, Boris couldn't get out the passenger door since it was jammed shut. Boris was looking toward Kirell for some assistance as to what he should do. Kirell directed him to slide over the console and come out the driver's door.

As Kirell waited for his partner in crime, he started assessing the situation. He could see the red lights from the police cars lined up on the street. On the driver's side of the Bentley there were no cops but just darkened houses. In order to blend into the neighborhood, he ripped off his ski mask and dropped it on the ground next to the driver's door. He knew that he needed to escape before the cops surrounded the car.

He could see Boris crawling out of the Bentley and he copied Kirell and pulled off his ski mask and threw it on the vehicle's floorboard. He tried to stand up but gave out a loud moan. Kirell yelled at him to follow him as he ran across the side yard of the house. He could see Boris leaning over as he ran behind him. When Kirell reached a cinder block wall he took his hand to reach the top of the wall. With his adrenaline on high he was able to pull himself over the wall.

Kirell fell down on the other side and got up on his knees and pulled himself up. He turned back to see if Boris had made it but saw no one. At that moment he knew that he had to save himself first and help his homie second. Since he could hear more police units arriving at the crash site, he needed to get out of there in lightning speed. He had to assume that Boris could take care of himself.

Kirell spent more than an hour discussing the facts of the case with the detective and prosecutor. Kirell started to go off topic by inquiring about his crime partner Boris. He directly asked the detective about the status of Boris' trial. After he was told that it was pending, he asked whether the police had been able to link Boris to the crime by DNA evidence. They didn't want to go into specifics about what evidence they had against Boris.

Kirell with a sly smile said that he would have gotten away with the robbery if it wasn't for the DNA on the ski mask. It was clear that Kirell was proud of his accomplishment in pulling off the Rawlings robbery with all of its planning and shrewd execution. He continually bragged that he would have gotten away with it if it hadn't been for his DNA showing up in the ski mask. He kept harping on the fact that he originally was sure he was going to get away with the crime. The detective and deputy DA leaned back in their chairs wondering what they were missing in the reasoning of Kirell's thinking.

Then Kirell started on the blame game claiming that it was Boris' fault for leaving the duct tape on the ground outside the garage. He went so far as to tell them that he was planning to kill Boris. As a matter of fact, Kirell claimed that he actually reached down under his seat in order to grab the gun to shoot Boris. However, after the crash he was more interested in helping Boris get out of the car since he didn't want Boris to be around to later snitch on him.

After a long and detailed interview, the detective and the prosecutor thanked Kirell for the first-hand account of the facts of the case. However, the $64,000 question was why Kirell was turning on his fellow gang member and partner in crime. Obviously, there was some type of falling out between the two homies. The prosecutor started thinking if she should use Kirell as a witness in Boris' trial. Since he would be considered an accomplice that meant everything he said had to be corroborated.

CHAPTER 21- PREPARING FOR BORIS' JURY TRIAL

Since it took so long for Boris' trial to start, the assigned trial prosecutor had to be changed. The original prosecutor was Shelly Samuels. Since Kirell's trial in 1999, she had been assigned the Robert Blake case. It was a publicity case that seemed to be continually delayed by the defendant firing and hiring new attorneys. The judge in the Robert Blake case grew tired of all the Defense delays so the judge ordered that the Blake case would start trial on a specific date. Subsequently both Blake and Boris Graham cases were scheduled to start at the same time. The result was another prosecutor would have to be brought in at the last minute to try the Boris Graham case.

When a new prosecutor is assigned to a case it can be disruptive. This Boris Graham case wasn't a simple case. Since Shelly Samuels had been assigned to the DA's Major Crimes Division, it fell upon the head deputy of that Division, Pat Dixon, to determine who should be the unlucky recipient of such a complex case. Most of the heavy hitters in Major Crimes were tied up in protracted cases that were actually in trial.

Although Beth Silverman had a full load of major cases, she was the type of attorney who couldn't say 'no' to another homicide case. She was one of those people who had a 'can do attitude.' Although she is a methodical person, she doesn't dwell on the obstacles that she will have to overcome. Her self-confidence allows her to take on anything with the realization that at a later time she will be able to figure out how to solve any problem she is confronted with.

When Beth was asked if she could do the Boris Graham trial her answer was, "Isn't it a San Fernando Valley case." What that meant was that Beth considered herself a 'Valley Girl.' Although she was really a 'Calabasas Girl,' she somehow had adopted the entire San Fernando Valley as her turf. After finishing law school and passing the bar exam she spent time law clerking for the Los Angeles DA's Office. Your author was instrumental in hiring Beth Silverman as a deputy district attorney. Since she was familiar with the San Fernando Valley, she was assigned to both the Van Nuys Courthouse and the San Fernando Courthouse. Over the years she earned a repudiation of fighting crime and attempting to make the San Fernando Valley a safer place to live. She seemed to have a personal stake in ridding the San Fernando Valley of criminals and neer-do-wells.

As soon as the Boris Graham case was transferred to Beth, she began to immerse herself into learning the facts of the case. It wasn't long before Beth visited the Trial Support Division asking me, the author, what we could do for her in the short amount of time she had to prepare for this case. While Beth was talking to me, she had a stack of police reports and crime scene photos clutched in her hands. I motioned her to go over to one of the empty layout tables. She started spreading everything out over the table and without wasting a moment of time she began talking. She pointed to the photos of Christopher and Lorie Rawlings and explained how the two of them were involved in the case.

In short order, I comprehended that Christopher had been unfortunately killed in an auto crash and Lorie survived by using her quick wit. Then Beth shifted gears and started explaining the roles of the two suspects. At that point she tossed on the table a photo of Boris and said this is the dude she was going to have to try. She alluded to the other suspect, Kirell, and explained his role in the crime and that he had been already convicted. Beth made this off-handed comment that she was hoping to use him as a witness in her trial.

At that point I was nodding my head in agreement to what Beth was saying but started to realize I didn't truly understand what each suspect had done during the crime. Beth is so mentally nimble that it can be a challenge to keep up with her thinking. I raised up my hand to indicate to Beth that I was getting lost. She smiled because she recognized that she was firing out the facts like a machine gun and she needed to slow down so I could absorb what she was saying. Beth is extremely bright yet she is smart enough to know when she needed to reduce the speed of her rhetoric in order to communicate with the jurors.

She had learned to use visual aids as a way to force herself to diminish her pace so jurors could follow along. Beth has the unique talent to focus the jurors' attention on the relevant facts of a case and paint a picture of the entire case for the jurors. She is described by some as being a great storyteller. Over the years she has honed her skills to know how to communicate the facts to the jurors so they understand them but most of all they remember those facts. Her Opening Statement to the jury reminds one of a contractor who likes to lay a solid foundation before building the structure.

She uses her Opening Statement to cement into the jurors' minds the facts of the case and the interconnection of those facts to one another. In order to effectively accomplish this, she uses a short PowerPoint slide show that provides the backdrop to what she is orally explaining to the jurors. Since I had worked with Beth on numerous Opening Statement slide shows, I had a good idea what she wanted. The only problem was could we prepare a slideshow within the short amount of time she had before she had to start the trial.

After listening to Beth for over an hour I began to sketch out what she would need for her Opening Statement. Then I asked her what facts she wanted inserted into the various slides. She explained she wanted to introduce the jurors to the Rawlings family by showing a photo of Christopher and Lorie with a picture of their home. She wanted the jurors to feel like this could have happened to any one of them. After preparing a number of slides I again met with Beth to go over the order of the slides. After several attempts I had Beth's Opening Statement ready for her first day of trial. Her first slide of her Opening Statement spelled out the basic facts that the jurors needed to know with the defendant's name and the case number of the case. That was followed by the slide showing Christopher and Lorie Rawlings with a photo of their Woodland Hills house.

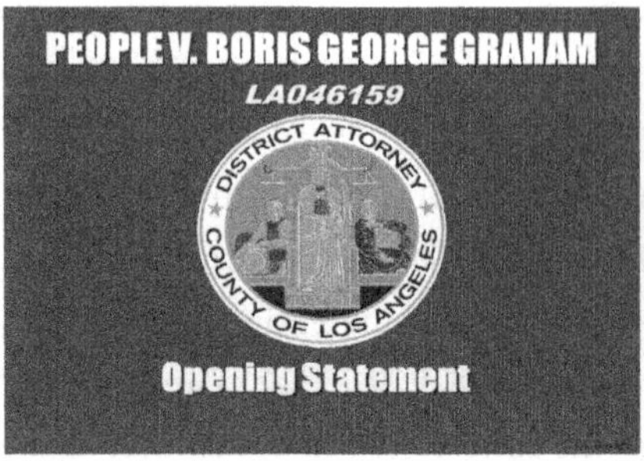

After this brief introduction Beth wanted the jury to understand why Christopher was the prime target because he always wore fine jewelry. Wearing such expensive jewelry and driving a flashy Bentley made him a potential victim in the eyes of the robbers in the San Fernando Valley. That slide was followed by showing the Rawlingses' garage. Included on that slide was the laundry room door which Lorie opened to see the robbers in the garage.

Beth had some other slides showing the various rooms of the house. Then Beth had a slide made showing the interior of the Baby's room. This was important for the jurors to see how it was possible for her and the children to climb out onto the roof.

Since the taking of the jewelry was going to be important, Beth used a slide showing various pictures of the master Bedroom.

She wanted the jurors to see where Lorie's jewelry was taken from her jewelry box.

Next, she wanted the jury to understand the route of the pursuit. She used this map so the jury would understand where everything occurred. The next slide showed how the Bentley crashed into a large tree in the front yard of one of the residents on Tampa Avenue.

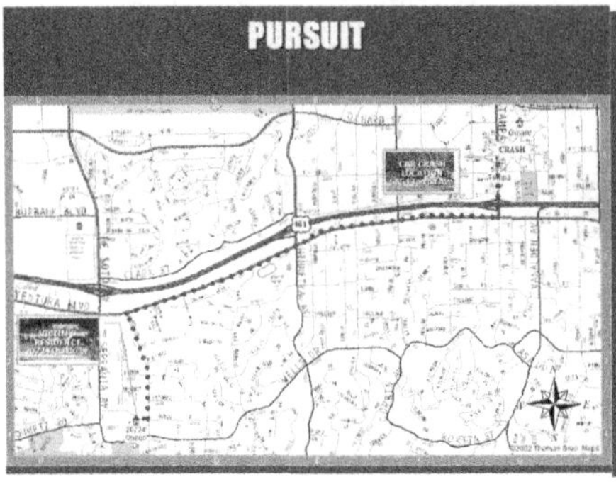

Beth knew she needed the jurors to understand exactly where the ski masks were found. She used four separate photos to show the area next to the driver's door of the Bentley. She used two red circles to clearly show where the one ski mask was on the driver's seat and the other on the ground. The other photos showed where the police scanner was found and where one of the gloves dropped on the ground.

Beth used her slide show in her Opening Statement to set the stage for the jury. The next step was to show the connection between all the people involved and their relationship to each other. In particular there were certain statements made by the various parties that the jurors needed to remember. She called this slide 'Corroboration of Taylor' since it showed all the key statements and who made them. Although the slide seemed to be too busy, Beth wanted the jurors to see on one page all the important people and their roles in the case. She couldn't afford to have the jurors become confused as to who did what and who said what.

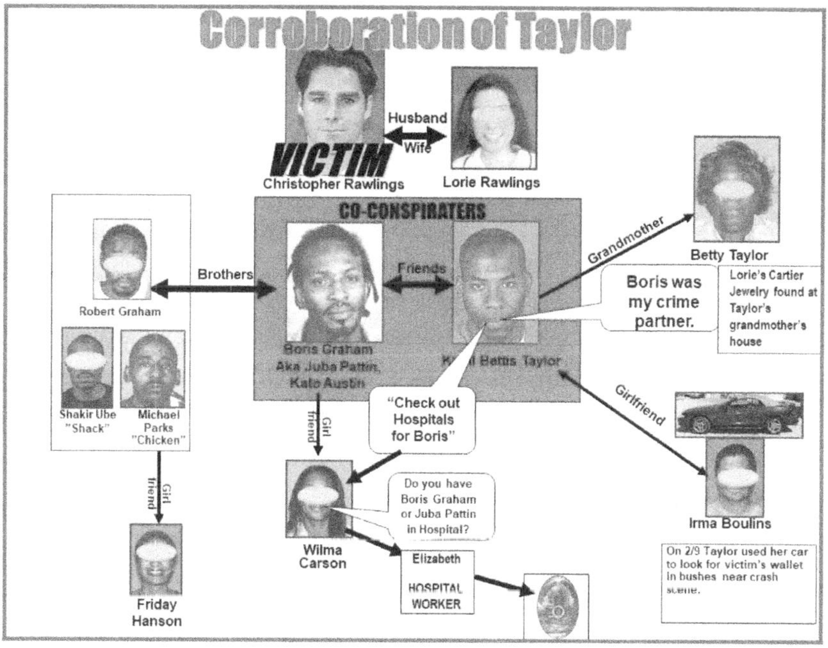

At the end of Beth's Opening Statement, she used two slides showing how the ski masks contained DNA from each of the ski masks. These slides showed all the details that proved that it was the suspects' DNA on the ski masks. Beth had the actual photos of the ski masks inserted on the slide as a photo of that particular defendant. She knew that she needed the jurors to understand the importance of this evidence which placed both Boris and Kirell in the Bentley at the time of the crash.

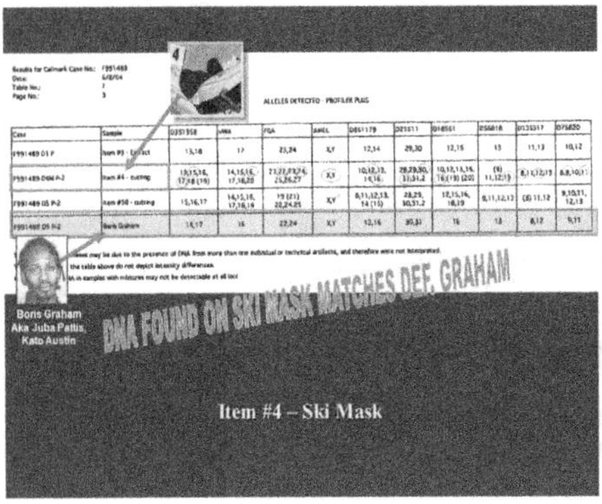

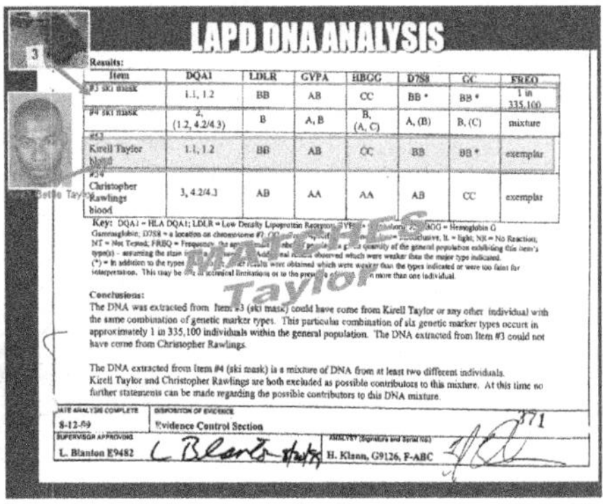

By the time Beth had finished her Opening Statement she had the jurors primed to do their job. She had laid out the facts in an understandable manner but her enormous challenge was whether she would be able to prove up all she had claimed. She knew that she was going to have to rely on hostile witnesses not knowing what they would actually say on the witnesses stand.

CHAPTER 22- BASIC WITNESSES FOR BORIS' TRIAL

Beth had completed her Opening Statement and now it was 'showtime' and she had to start calling her witnesses. She used her most effective witness who was Christopher's wife, **Lorie.** Beth knew that the jurors would love Lorie as a person. Beth never had a more sympathetic witness. How could the jurors not admire what Lorie had done to keep her children safe from the robbers? After the jurors had listened to Beth's Opening Statement, they seemed to have some type of human bond with Lorie.

Beth with a compassionate voice started questioning Lorie as to what happened on February 8, 1999. By now Lorie had testified so many times as to all the tragic events she could do it as though she were on auto-pilot. Since it was over six years since these dreadful events had happened, she really wished she could place this nightmare behind her. She had moved on with her life and her emphasis was on trying to provide a normal life for her children who were being forced to grow up without a father.

As Lorie started to testify, she hoped this would be the last time she was going to have to recite all the tragic facts that totally had changed her life. She explained to the jury that she was in her kitchen when she heard the automatic garage door open and could hear the Bentley drive in. The loud music from the car radio didn't concern her since her husband always played it loud. However, what caught her attention was the hearing of at least two loud, stern unfamiliar voices. She walked over to the slightly open door between the kitchen and laundry room and peered into the garage.

She could see her husband on his knees on the ground and two men, dressed "head to toe" in black, holding or pushing her husband down. From where she was standing, she could see the Bentley's trunk was open. At that point, she explained to the jurors that she turned and very quietly retraced her steps back through the laundry room into the kitchen. She described how she went over to the cordless phone and grabbed it. Then she immediately gathered her older child and went upstairs.

She used the phone to dial 9-1-1 and told a police dispatcher what was happening. Then she went into detail how she was able to place both of her children on the ledge outside of the window. The women on the juror were mesmerized as Lorie showed them on a photo exhibit where she was perched on the roof. The female jurors seemed to be in a state of shock when they could see how narrow the roof ledge was. The minds of those jurors undoubtedly thought to themselves what would they have done under the same conditions.

Lorie explained that her senses were in overload. She was trying to keep her children quiet while they clung precariously on the ledge. At the same time, she was listening to a lot of scuffling of items being moved around. Most of the time she couldn't make out what the people were doing in the house but they seemed to be noisy. While attempting to listen to the robbers, she was in constant contact with the police dispatcher. She tried to answer the dispatcher's request for more information by talking softly not to attract attention of the robbers especially when they went through the Baby's room.

The dispatcher tried to reassure Lorie that police units were responding. It seemed like an eternity for Lorie as she was crouched down on the ledge of the roof. She explained that she wanted to remain calm for the sake of her children who were looking at mommy with uncontrollable fear. She stated to the jury that the voices seemed to grow fainter until she heard a blood-curdling scream which seemed to be from her husband.

She related that the next sound she heard was the garage door opening directly beneath her. As she looked down from the roof to the driveway, she saw the Bentley slowly backing out of the garage. She tried to see who was in the car but couldn't make out who was inside. When the car bumped the curb on the other side of the street, she knew that the driver wasn't her husband. Her husband would never have backed out hitting the curb since he was so overly protective of his Bentley.

She explained that she could make out the outline of a police car further down the street. She testified that within minutes she had crawled back inside the house as the other officers were examining the house. Lorie related that when she checked out the master bedroom, she found it had been completely ransacked. Items missing were a blue-faced Rolex watch and Cartier bracelet and earrings. When she went downstairs, she noticed an orange juice container was resting on the kitchen counter. She also saw that her purse had been emptied out on the small table and she promptly noticed her wallet was missing.

The next phase of Lorie's testimony involved going to see her husband in the Northridge Hospital where he died two days later from the head injuries he suffered during the crash. By then the prosecutor was finished with her direct examination. It was time for Boris' attorney to cross-examine Lorie. Boris' female Defense attorney was smart enough to realize that any attacking of the widow of the murder victim was a losing proposition. The Defense attorney knew that Lorie had the jurors glued to her testimony. They were sympathetic towards her. The Defense attorney's main objective was to get Lorie off the witness stand as quickly as possible.

The next set of prosecution witnesses were the responding officers to the Rawlings house. They testified that they approached the house and waited on the side of the garage. From that location they saw the Bentley roll down the driveway and hit the curb. Afterward they explained that they entered the house and on the second floor found Lorie and the children coming in through the infant's room window. These officers didn't add much to proving that Boris was involved in the robbery.

The next witnesses were the pursuing officers who initially chased the Bentley. They stated that the Bentley was pulling away from them even though they were traveling nearly a 110 miles per hour. However, it was another set of officers who testified that they were responding to a radio broadcast and they noticed a white Bentley was headed in their direction. The car came toward them at a high rate of speed and proceeded northbound on Tampa Avenue. They activated their lights and siren and broadcasted that they were pursuing the Bentley.

Before they could gain on the Bentley, they saw the Bentley hit a blue vehicle which spun into a power pole knocking it down. The Bentley subsequently went out of control spinning around and skidding into another power pole. They described how the Bentley came to rest wrapped around a large tree in the front yard of one of the houses. Initially there were crashing sounds that immediately turned into a shower of sparks from the live electric lines falling onto the Bentley. Moments later the street lights went dark as well as the lights in the adjoining houses. The officers noticed flames coming from the engine compartment of the Bentley. The officers used their flashlights to illuminate the crash site and could see that the trunk lid was open.

Since they had been told that there might be a hostage, one of the officers shined his flashlight into the trunk and found it to be empty. He followed a pattern of debris on the ground from the vehicle's trunk to a block wall, where he saw an adult male on the ground next to the wall. He saw blood on the wall which he surmised came from the victim hitting it.

The detective who responded to the crash site testified to shining his flashlight into the interior of the Bentley. There he noticed a ski mask on the driver's seat and another one on the ground next to the driver's door. He also saw a police scanner, as well as a glove on the ground. Moments later he found a pair of open handcuffs against the wall near where the blood was found on the block wall. This witness laid the foundation for the forensic evidence which would later be used to connect Boris to the ski mask.

Next the jurors heard testimony from several civilian witnesses who lived in the area of the crash site. They basically testified to seeing a black man prowling through their backyards and even some stated that they tried to chase him. That concluded the testimony as to the events that took place the night of the crime and the pursuit that resulted in the crash.

The next witness was Jack Mayes who testified that he lived a block away from the crash site. When he went to retrieve his van the following morning, he found a pile of black clothing lying on the street between two vehicles. He thought it was strange, especially after all the police activity the night before. He notified the police and an officer came by to pick up the clothing as possible evidence.

Donna Colliers testified next and explained to the jury that she was driving past the intersection of Wilbur and Calvert Street when she noticed a green car with a tan top parked in the right-hand traffic lane. This caught her attention as she watched a tall black man appear to be searching through the bushes. This seemed curious to her so she continued to observe the man who seemed to be frantically looking for something under the bushes. She knew about the crash of the Bentley and remembered that the neighbors claimed they saw two black men run away.

After several minutes of searching the area the man got back in the Mustang and drove off. Ms. Colliers told the jury she didn't know what to make of the odd activity. She notified the police of her observations and shortly thereafter she met with a Detective Weston. She showed the detective where the man was standing when he was rummaging through the bushes. She remained at the location with the detective as he looked through the landscaping. Then she saw him lean over and pick up a man's wallet. The detective looked through the wallet and mentioned to her that the wallet contained Mr. Rawlings' identification.

Detective Weston was the next witness explaining that he recovered the wallet from the area where Ms. Colliers had pointed out to him. He told the jury that he had earlier picked up the clothing discovered by Mr. Mayes. When he examined the sweatshirt, he noticed there was duct tape attached to the clothing.

Beth had tried so many homicide cases that she knew how difficult it was to obtain the actual medical examiner from the Coroner's Office who had performed the autopsy. They were either tied up performing autopsies or testifying in another murder trial. When Beth's witness coordinator told her that the medical examiner would be available in the afternoon, Beth decided to call him out of order to assure she got his testimony. Occasionally when the actual medical examiner who performed the autopsy isn't available, the prosecutor can call another medical examiner to testify to the autopsy report. Beth didn't want to use a substitute medical examiner. She wanted the jurors to hear from the medical examiner who in fact cut the victim open explain first-hand what he discovered.

Beth understood her role as a communicator in the courtroom. She knew that the jurors were fascinated in seeing and hearing a real coroner. Most jurors have seen on television or the movies how coroners are depicted. Some remembered Jack Klugman playing the role as the coroner in the TV series "Quincy."

Beth knew that there was a fine line between educating the jurors and grossing them out. Although the shock and awe approach can be captivating, it also can turn some jurors off who mentally tune out and miss the crucial meaning of the medical examiner's testimony. Beth had learned that the jurors are captivated when listening to the medical examiner describe how he or she performed the autopsy.

The autopsy of Christopher Rawlings wasn't anything out of the ordinary. Beth needed the medical examiner to explain that Christopher died from blunt force trauma. Since Christopher didn't die immediately, she needed the medical examiner to testify that in his opinion the blunt force trauma occurred when the victim struck his head against the cinder block wall after being thrown from the trunk of the car.

Beth showed the medical examiner an exhibit including four photos of Christopher's head. She walked the medical examiner through each photo so he could point out what part of Christopher's skull was fractured. Although the photos were graphic, Beth guided the medical examiner through them as though he were teaching a medical school class. The jurors listened intently as though this was vital evidence.

In order to prove the actual cause of death, Beth showed the medical examiner several poster size diagrams that the medical examiner had filled out at the time of the autopsy. These diagrams better illustrated how and where Christopher's skull was fractured. Although the one diagram looked more like a head of a skeleton, it was easier for the jurors to see that the victim had suffered a massive head injury.

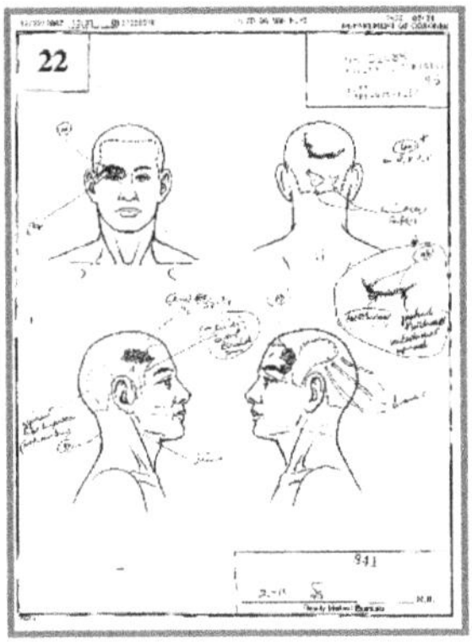

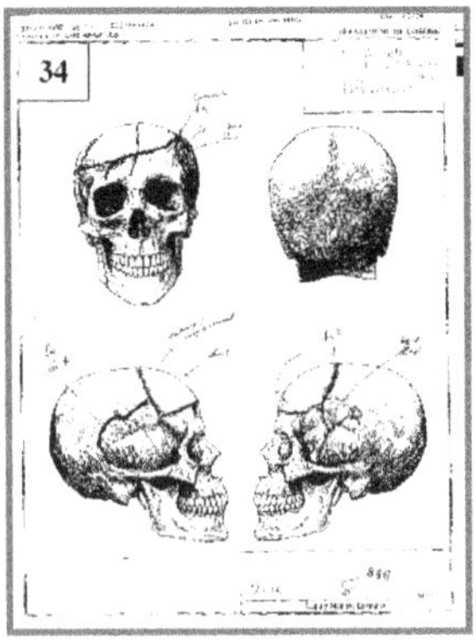

CHAPTER 23- TESTIMONY OF DETECTIVE POWELL

Beth was glad to finish up the medical examiner's testimony so she could concentrate on her difficult witnesses. In order to lay the proper foundation, she called **Detective Powell** the lead detective. He started out by telling the jury that he and Detective Weston arrived at the Rawlings house at 11:10 p.m. to conduct an investigation regarding the stolen property that had been taken by the residential robbers. When they arrived, Detective Powell went into the kitchen where he noticed an open gallon container of orange juice on the kitchen counter. He also explained that a female's purse had been overturned with its contents scattered on a small kitchen table.

He further testified about going upstairs and seeing a jewelry box open with drawers pulled out and tipped upside down. Later he talked to Lorie who described the items that were missing. She mentioned that one of her husband's Rolex watches had been taken from the bedroom. She agreed to find out the serial number for that watch. As to the missing Cartier jewelry, she indicated that she would supply photos of the items which had been taken and when the items were purchased.

He related to the jury that when he was surveying the exterior of the property, he noticed a new role of duct tape near the right side of the garage door. He had it retrieved and marked for evidence.

He went on to explain that he went to the tow yard to check on the Bentley. While looking through the interior of the car, he found and recovered a loaded revolver on the passenger side floorboard. In addition, Lorie's wallet was found near the revolver. Later they examined the car trunk where he recovered the remote-control garage door opener which had a blood stain across the face of it.

As to the ski masks he didn't recover them from the Bentley but they had been recovered by the CSI team at the crash site. Detective Powell explained to the jury that he didn't know if the Crime Lab could extract cellular material around the mouth area of the mask. Eventually he had the LAPD Scientific Division try to find a sufficient amount of material for testing. When they believed they had enough he directed them to send the samples to the CellMark lab that performed the DNA testing.

Then Detective Powell started telling the jury about the investigation focusing on Kirell Taylor. He explained that he conducted a surveillance of Kirell's residence on Vaughn Street. While doing this he noticed a green Mustang convertible with a tan top parked in front of the house. That car was identical to the one Ms. Colliers had seen parked in the street where a man frantically was looking for something in the bushes. The detective took down the license number and later determined that the registered owner was Kirell's girlfriend, Irma Bijous.

The detective further testified that he obtained a search warrant for Kirell's residence. When he went into Kirell's bedroom he recovered a Cartier bracelet and one earring from a pair of Cartier earrings. Later he showed the items to Lorie who was able to identify them as the ones taken from her house. The detective went on to say that he recovered a Koran at the foot of Kirell's bed. When he opened the book he found on one page a business card for Rawlings' store, Gentleman's Quarters, in the name of Rodney Leonard.

Detective Powell continued to testify that he obtained another search warrant for Kirell's girlfriend's Mustang. He explained that in the trunk of the Mustang were documents connecting Kirell to using this Mustang. One was a traffic citation written to Kirell while he was driving the Mustang.

The next few questions the detective was asked pertained to him seeing an Illinois driver's license with a photo of Boris Graham on it, although it was in the name of a Kato Austin.

CHAPTER 24 KIRELL TESTIFIED

Beth had an easy task of questioning Detective Powell compared to the next witness who she was about to question. Then Beth called **Kirell Taylor** as her next witness. Kirell had freely talked to Detective Powell at the state prison, however, Kirell had a change of heart. Now Kirell didn't want to testify against his old homie. This change of heart by Kirell placed Beth in a odd situation. She, as a prosecutor, would be calling a witness who she knew wasn't going to tell the truth. When Kirell was called to the witness stand, the courtroom clerk asked him to raise his right hand and then stated, "You swear to tell the truth the whole truth and nothing but the truth so help you God." At the end, Kirell put his head down and muttered the word "Yah" and just slouched into the witness chair.

Many people believe that when a witness takes an oath to tell the truth they in fact are telling the truth. That may be wishful thinking. Some people believe that a lying witness will be charged with perjury if he or she isn't truthful. However, in the real world there is seldom anything done when a witness lies. In my 43 years as a prosecutor, I can remember only two times when charges of perjury were filed against a deceitful witness.

As Kirell sat down in the witness chair the prosecutor asked him if he told Detective Powell during a prison interview that he and Boris committed a residential Robbery of Christopher Rawlings. Kirell fired back by saying that those were all lies. Then he was asked if his conversation with the detective and the prosecutor was tape recorded. He acknowledged that it was. Then Beth asked if he had said during the recording that he and Boris had committed the Rawlings robbery-murder. His immediate response was that it was all bogus. He vehemently claimed that his inculpating of Boris in the Robbery were all lies. To emphases his disclaimer he said that he did not even know Boris until 1998.

Generally a prosecutor doesn't call witnesses who are outright liars. However, the law does permit a prosecutor or any attorney to call a witness who previously made prior inconsistent statements which the attorney believes were truthful. Thus prior inconsistent statements can be used to prove a fact in a case.

After Kirell had testified in front of the jury claiming that everything he had told the detective was a lie, Beth finished up telling the court, "No more questions." This allowed Boris' Defense attorney to ask Kirell to reiterate that everything he had said in the interview was a bold face lie. The jurors had skeptical looks on their faces as to what to make of Kirell the so-called 'Prosecution Witness.'

Without missing a beat Beth recalled Detective Powell to the witness stand. Beth asked him if he had any contact with Kirell after he was convicted and sentenced to Life without the possibility of parole in state prison. Detective Powell related to the jury that years later after Kirell's conviction he received a letter from Kirell who stated he wanted to provide information about his crime partner Boris Graham. Detective Powell made the arrangements to interview Kirell with the original prosecutor Shelly Samuels.

Powell further testified that on September 21, 2006, he and the prosecutors met with Kirell at the state prison where he was being housed. As they sat down in an interview room, the detective removed a tape recorder from his briefcase and placed it on the table in front of Kirell and he pushed the button to record. Powell wasn't going to ask permission to record the conversation, but placed Kirell on noticed that anything he said was being recorded. This may have caught Kirell by surprise but since he was the person who had called this meeting together it was too late for him to object to the recording.

Beth asked the detective if he had a tape recording of the interview. He authenticated the tape for the court and indicated that the tape had been transcribed. He was asked if he had reviewed the transcription to see if it was accurate. He replied that he had and had found the transcription to be correct and complete.

Beth asked him to relate to the jury the highlights of the interview. He began by asking basic questions of Kirell such as how well he knew Boris. Kirell told him that he had grown up with Boris in the Pacoima area. He also knew Michael Parks and Irma Bijoux who lived in the neighborhood. After Kirell explained his relationship with the various parties, he was asked for his version as to the facts of the residential robbery of the Rawlingses.

(You the reader have already read in a previous chapter what Kirell told Detective Powell and the prosecutor. In this chapter we will highlight a few of the items that were discussed during the interview at the state prison.)

Kirell started out telling Powell that his girlfriend, Irma Bijoux had dropped off Boris and himself at the Rawlings residence in her green Mustang. Kirell went on to described how they surprised the victim as he got out of his Bentley. Kirell further explained that they had brought along handcuffs to immobilize Mr. Rawlings. He related that their objective was to rob the residents especially to find the safe where the valuables were kept. They planned on carjacking this luxurious vehicle as a bonus.

Detective Powell told the jury that the interview took an odd turn when Kirell inquired as to what type of evidence they had against his crime partner, Boris. He was mainly interested in knowing if the DA had Boris' DNA evidence on the other ski mask. For a moment the interview of Kirell seemed to drift off topic.

Then the detective redirected Kirell back on track as to the facts of the case. Kirell went into detail as to what the two of them did. He described how they move up to the master bedroom where he saw Boris take items of jewelry from a jewelry box as well as pick up a Rolex watch on the dresser.

Kirell related that they all returned downstairs and Boris escorted the victim back into the garage while he surveyed the kitchen area. Moments later Kirell heard the victim screaming and he rushed back to the garage where he saw Boris pointing the gun at the victim's head.

At that point Boris began searching Mr. Rawlings for items to take. He took the easy items like the Rolex and gold bracelet, then they heard over the scanner that the police were converging on the victim's house. In order to make their 'getaway' they pushed the victim into the trunk and slammed it shut. Both guys jumped into the Bentley and they backed the car down the driveway.

At that point Detective Powell told the jury that Kirell provided the details of the pursuit. He drove at a high rate of speed down to Ventura Boulevard. It wasn't until he struck a blue car that he lost control of the Bentley.

Beth wanted Powell to explain to the jury the strangest part of this conversation. She asked the detective if Kirell made any statement about what he was going to do with his crime partner Boris. Powell turned to face the jurors and related that Kirell had planned to kill his homie Boris. He state that he actually reached down under the driver's seat and grabbed his gun. Kirell said he didn't want to leave Boris to be a snitch against him. However, when he noticed that Boris seemed shaken up from the crash, he had a change of heart and decided to help Boris climb out of the mangled car.

The jurors attentively listened to Detective Powell testify as to what Kirell had said during the interview. They must have been confused as to why Kirell had told them from the witness stand that none of what he had said to the detective was true even though it was recorded. The jurors had to ponder why Kirell made all those incriminating statements against his old crime partner. What did Kirell have to gain?

CHAPTER 25- PARKS TESTIMONY AT BORIS' TRIAL

The jurors must have been in a state of confusion after hearing Kirell's testimony in which he claimed he hadn't been truthful in his interview with Detective Powell. The next prosecution witness was **Michael Parks** who would take a similar approach. Mr. Parks would deny making any incriminating statements against Boris or Kirell, however this time Detective Powell wouldn't have a tape recording of the conversation since Parks hadn't permitted the interview to be recorded. Park's condition for a tape recording was that if the police helped him out with his pending case in Chicago then they could record it. Since the Cook County DA wouldn't agree to any deal in Parks' case, there was no tape recording.

This time the jurors would have to rely on Detective Powell's notes and memory as to what Michael Parks had told him. When Beth called Michael Parks to the witness stand, she didn't know how honest his testimony would be. Beth initiated the questioning with a simple inquiry by asking Parks if knew Boris Graham. To that question Parks freely admitted knowing Boris. He said they grew up to in the same Pacoima neighborhood. He had known Boris for over 25 years and knew him by the name Booney. He explained that in May of 1999, he received a call from Boris who asked if he and his friend Shake could come to Chicago to stay for a short time. Parks agreed that they could stay with him at his mother's house. He realized that would make it extremely crowded since his girlfriend Friday Hanson was also staying with him and his mother. The reason he did this was to help out an old friend from the 'hood.'

The prosecutor was pleased that Parks wasn't going to claim that he didn't know Boris or hadn't seen him in years. But the next line of questioning caused Parks to become evasive and he wouldn't say anything that was incriminating toward Boris. When Parks was asked if he had ever told the detectives that Boris and Kirell had gone to a rich guy's house to steal money and drugs from a safe, he adamantly denied saying that. Beth asked further questions about the Rawlings residential robbery as to Boris telling him that he and Kirell threw the rich guy into the trunk of his car. Parks shook his head denying ever saying that. He continued to repudiate ever telling the detectives that Boris told him that there was a police pursuit and that they crashed the Roll Royce (Parks used that term even though it was a Bentley). He further denied that Boris told him that when the car crashed the victim was "spit out of the trunk" and killed.

The prosecutor was disappointed but not surprised that Parks wasn't going to be candid. She wanted to get several more things out of him in front of the jury. She asked whether he had helped Boris get a driver's license in Chicago. For some reason he was willing to admit that he let Boris use his mother's car to take the driver's license test. Further he remembered Boris got the license in the name of Kato Austin. When the prosecutor asked about whether he knew Kirell, this witness became even more evasive.

The prosecutor had gotten as much as she could from this hostile witness. Both Kirell and Michael Parks had been extremely difficult witnesses for Beth. Most people would rather have had a double root canal without Novocaine than try to get these old homies to tell the truth on the witness stand. Beth was now going to have to totally rely on Detective Powell's testimony of what Boris told Parks to prove up Park's prior inconsistent statements. This is when the prosecutor dearly wished she had a tape recording of that conversation.

After Michael Parks had testified Beth again recalled Detective Powell and started asking him questions about what Parks had told him regarding what Boris told him about his involvement in the Rawlings robbery-murder. Beth first asked Detective Powell how he became aware of Michael Parks. The detective explained that he had received information that a Michael Parks was a suspect in the Rawlings murder.

Powell explained to the jury that he learned that Parks was in custody in Chicago. On September 15, 1999, he went to the Cook County Jail and interviewed Michael Parks. Then Detective Powell showed Parks two separate six-pack photo line-ups which contained a photo of Boris Graham in one and in the other a photo of Kirell Taylor. Powell said that was when Parks smiled at him and said, "This is what this is all about, the mother fucker Booney."

The detective continued to tell the jury that Parks acknowledged that he knew Boris to be Booney and he had come to Chicago to stay with him. He told the detective that Boris admitted that he and Kirell were involved in a home invasion robbery where he stole a "Rolls Royce" and they threw the male owner into the trunk. Boris told Parks that there was a police pursuit in which they crashed the car into a tree and the collision caused the victim to be 'spit out' of the trunk.

Detective Powell explained to the jury that at that point Parks was claiming to have obtained a confession from Boris. Parks went on to say that his girlfriend Friday Hanson was present on several occasions when Boris bragged about committing this residential robbery. In order to verify what Parks was saying Detective Powell contacted Parks' girlfriend and she corroborated what Parks was saying about Boris being involved in the Rawlings case.

Detective Powell indicated to the jury that as a result of obtaining these oral statements from both Parks and his girlfriend he decided to request a criminal complaint be filed against Boris Graham for the robbery and murder of Christopher Rawlings. On September 23, 1999, the DA's Office filed a complaint against Boris Graham as well as obtained a warrant for his arrest. At that time the police had no idea of the whereabouts of Boris Graham and the warrant was placed in the national warrant database. It wasn't until almost four years later on January 28, 2004, that Boris Graham was arrested on the warrant.

CHAPTER 26 FRIDAY TELLS THE TRUTH

Beth's next witness was Parks' girlfriend Friday Hanson. Would she tell the truth in court about overhearing Boris admitting to committing the Rawlings killing? However, the prosecutor's faith in humanity took an upward turn when she called Parks' girlfriend Friday Hanson. She testified that she was present during a conversation among Boris, Shake and Parks. She remembered Boris saying he had participated in a home invasion robbery with Kirell. She went on to say that Boris stated that they believed that there was a safe in the house that contained valuables and possibly drugs. She recalled Boris saying the robbery went awry because the victim's wife called 9-1-1. The best Miss Hanson could recollect, Boris stated they kidnapped a wealthy man who lived in Bel Air or Beverly Hills and placed him in the trunk of a Rolls Royce or a Bentley. Boris explained that there was a high-speed chase with the police and they crashed into a brick wall.

As a result of the crash the kidnapped man flew out of the trunk. Boris went on to say they took off their ski masks and escaped into the neighborhood. Shortly after the incident his partner was caught by the police. Boris continued to explain that the police obtained Kirell's DNA from sweat or saliva from the ski mask and used it against Kirell at his trial.

Of course, Parks' girlfriend had gotten a few of the facts mixed up but that was the way she remembered the conversations which had taken place over five years earlier. Why was this young woman willing to tell the truth? We will never know. Maybe she is one of those people who believe that when you take an oath to tell the truth that's what you do. How was her moral compass different from Kirell and Parks who both refused to tell the truth on the witness stand?

Friday Hanson's testimony was going to be crucial to the outcome of this case.

CHAPTER 27- WHAT'S DNA EVIDENCE ALL ABOUT?

By this time in the trial, Beth knew that the jurors were 100% convinced that the DA had proved the elements of robbery and murder but what she needed was some strong evidence to prove that Boris Graham was one of the criminals committing those crimes. The best way to do this was by using forensic evidence. With forensics the jurors don't have to decide who was telling the truth. Forensic evidence doesn't rely on the credibility of a witness but rested entirely on a scientific test that showed either a positive or negative result.

Prosecutors like it when they have forensic evidence, but unfortunately not all criminal cases leave a trail of scientific cracker crumbs leading to the criminal. Fortunately, in this present case Detective Powell was astute enough to have the ski masks analyzed for possible DNA results. Fortuitously, the Crime Lab was able to extract enough cellular material such as dried saliva and human tissue from around the edge of the mouth portion of both ski masks. Then it was up to CellMark to see if they could obtain a DNA result from the samples.

Beth was pleased that they had received positive results; however, it would take an incredible amount of work to prove everything up in court. Beth knew from first-hand experience she needed to build a solid foundation for the DNA evidence. When using forensic evidence, the prosecutor has to take on the role of a high school science teacher in order for certain jurors to be willing to rely on this form of scientific evidence. It only takes one juror to reject this type of forensic evidence to end up with a mistrial.

For a prosecutor, he or she has to convince all 12 jurors that the concept of using DNA to prove the identity of the criminal is acceptable evidence. Beth understood that all jurors come into the courtroom with various educational backgrounds and levels of worldly experience. The prosecutor has to be careful not to appear to talk down to the jurors. However, the prosecutor has to make sure that all the jurors are on board and willing to consider the DNA evidence.

Since Beth had tried so many cases involving DNA, she had learned how much she needed to teach the jurors as to DNA. Most people have some type of threshold that they need to learn about before they are willing to accept it as a scientific fact. An example is a computer. Most people couldn't describe how a computer actually works. However, they are willing to accept the results of the computer.

The same is true with DNA. How much background do the jurors need to know about DNA? On the next few pages we will be discussing DNA. The task for the prosecutor is to know how much of this following information about DNA needs to be explained to the jurors.

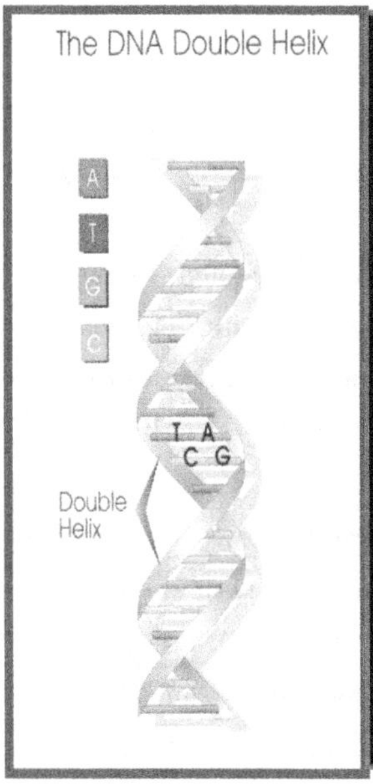

The following is an introduction to DNA being used in a criminal case. Back in 1953 scientists were trying to figure out what made up the basis for life. Several scientists in England by the name of Rosalind Franklin, Raymond Gosling and Maurice Wilkins discovered that by using X-ray diffraction they discovered that the DNA molecule was like a helix and resembled a ladder with rungs. Drawing upon that diffraction theory, two scientists named James Watson and Francis Crick determined that the structure of DNA was really a double-helix. Eventually in 1962, they were awarded the Nobel Prize for their contribution in unlocking the secrets of DNA.

After numerous experiments it was determined that all human cells contained DNA with the exception of red blood cells. Therefore, a person's DNA is the same in every white cell of their body. Each person's chromosome is made of genes. Part of the chromosome consists of detailed coding for various parts of the body. However, the other part of the chromosome is called 'junk' DNA. It is that junk portion that certain scientists became interested in since it was specific to each individual.

Not until 1984 did Alec Jeffreys discover a way of using 'junk' DNA to identify individuals. This became known as RFLP or 'DNA fingerprinting.' This method was named Multi-locus Probe in which the DNA is extracted from the cells by using a restrictive enzyme to fragment the DNA. Next electrophoresis separates the DNA fragments according to size. At that point a radioactive probe is added and binds to the specific DNA fragments.

The end result is autorads which are X-ray films with dark bands representing RFLP markers. The bands are found in lanes and each lane is this autorad contains DNA fragments from a different source. That spacing and thickness of the individual lines can be compared to tests from other individuals.

Below is an autorad showing a bloodstain sample in the center. On both sides are various samples from other suspects.

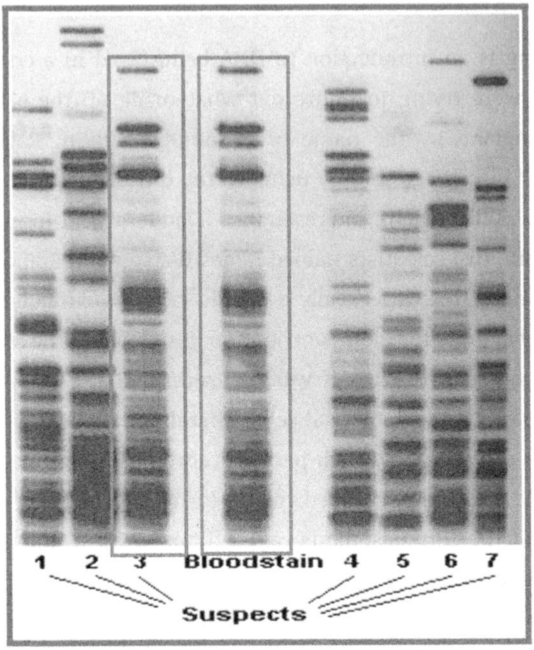

By comparing the bloodstain from the crime scene which is listed in the center with the other suspects, one can see that the horizontal lines for suspect #3 are similar to the lines from the crime scene bloodstain. The readers of the autorads have to use their eyes to decide whether there is a match.

This is a brief description of the DNA process and how it can be used to determine the identity of the original sample. It wasn't until 1986 that the concept was used in criminology. Several years earlier, two 15-year-old girls were raped and murdered in the area of Leicester, England. The first teenager was walking through an isolated area on the side of town when she was attacked and killed. There was no suspect apprehended and the community was growing concerned. Several months later another teenage girl was similarly attacked and killed. This second murder outraged the usually peaceful community and eventually there was a call for something to be done to catch the killer.

At about that time there was considerable discussion in the media and education institution indicating that scientists were capable of determining the identity of an individual from blood and other bodily fluids. People in the Leicester community were putting pressure on the police services to find a way to catch this killer. The investigators had obtained vaginal swabs from each of the victims.

The scientific community said that with the new technology they could extract the killer's DNA from the vaginal swabs. After considerable discussion law enforcement agreed to give over the swabs to a group that was working on the cutting edge of individual identification from DNA. After conducting several tests, the group believed that they had extracted sufficient DNA for testing.

CHAPTER 28- THE ENGLISH BLOODING

The next dilemma was how to go about obtaining a DNA sample from the suspect. Since both rape-murders occurred within a short distance of little village of Hinckley near Leicester, the authorities believed that the suspect most likely lived or worked in the immediate area. Back in 1986, there was no DNA database to compare the DNA results from the victims' vaginal swabs. At first law enforcement wanted to obtain DNA samples from local individuals who had a checkered past and had been previously arrested or convicted for some type of sexual assault. Certain people were called in by the authorities to provide a blood sample.

However, after a number of months and no DNA match, pressure was building for the leaders of the community to come up with a viable plan to catch the killer. Some people wanted the authorities to be more creative in their approach to apprehend the murderer. A plan was floated by some scientist that if the community was serious about catching the rapist strangler, then they should obtain a DNA sample from every person living in the area.

That radical idea received considerable resistance. Not everyone was convinced that such a mammoth dragnet was necessary or wise. But as the months moved on without the arrest of a suspect, the tide started to turn to try something radical. At that point the authorities seriously considered what part of the population should be included in such a massive community approach. That was when law enforcement was asked to describe the type of person that they believed committed this rape-murder.

Immediately it was agreed that the suspect would be a male who was sexually active. However, there wasn't a unanimous agreement as to what ages should be included in the definition of sexually active. Obviously very young boys were unlikely to be sexually active and it was agreed that they would include any male 14 years or older. Then they had to determine the upper age limit. They agreed that males older than 50 years were less likely to commit an offense of rape. However, after more reflection it was believed that the top age should be 40 years old.

By then the authorities had agreed that the age range should be14 to 40 for the group to be required to provide a DNA sample. The next issue was what should be the size of this geographic group. No one knew for certain what geographical area to be included. Should it be a five- or ten-mile radius from the location where the crimes occurred? The authorities didn't want the area to be too small and miss the suspect. On the hand they didn't want too large of an area and find that it would be impossible to analyze all the blood samples. Finally, the authorities came up with an arbitrary solution of making the distance to be a four-mile radius from the crime scenes.

What surprised many was the fact that in that geographical area there were 4,000 males between the ages of 14 to 40. In order to quell the dissent, it was decided that they would permit the sample to be by way of oral swabs instead of only blood samples. Many people have an aversion to people sticking needles in their body. So this compromise made the collection process much more amenable.

Next the authorities had to set up a system that would assure that all males who were included in the test group actually cooperated and submitted samples. At first it was a little chaotic trying to set up a place where the blood samples could be drawn. But leaving it to the Brits they figured out a way to obtain the necessary samples.

The next task was finding a way to analyze so many samples. Since nothing like this had been done on such a massive scale, the laboratory had to work overtime in order to test every sample. This herculean job was eventually finished. After the testing they needed to compare each of the samples with the DNA collected from the vaginal swabs. This was a laborious process of having an expert review the autorad of each sample with the autorads from the victims' vaginal swabs.

After months of tedious work, the experts found none of the samples to match up with the vaginal swabs. Not finding a suspect caused many to wonder whether the scientific groups had oversold the idea of individual identification. What could have gone wrong? Should they have included a larger group which might have included a 10-mile radius or males up to the age of 50? Since all this work had resulted in nothing, the criticism of the authorities could be expected. The feeling by many was that the DNA wasn't ready to be included as one of the gadgets in the criminology tool box.

As discouraged as the community leaders could be there was a surprising breakthrough. It all occurred in the most unlikely spot which turned out to be the sweet aroma of a bakery. Two bakers were working next to each other in the back baking room. They were making small talk among themselves. The topic somehow switched to the gigantic effort of obtaining every guy's blood sample. The one baker chuckled and said that he had given a sample in the name of Colin Pitchfork. The other worker asked why did you do that? His response was that Colin had some disputes with the police and was afraid that they would blame him for something else.

The two male workers laughed at how paranoid Colin had always been. They went on about their work not noticing several women who were working away preparing pastries for the bakery. After overhearing the guys talking two of the women looked at each other with a surprised look on their faces. Here they were merely bakery employees but they had a deep-seated concern for their community. They were much more suspicious of the conduct of Colin Pitchfork.

After lengthy debating back and forth it was decided that one of the women would contact the police. She didn't want to get their fellow baker colleague in trouble for lying to the police that he was Colin and providing a false sample. The one woman told the police that she had overheard that possibly Colin Pitchfork had not given a DNA sample.

The police didn't know what to make of this overheard conversation. Since the police were coming under intense criticism for not being able to catch the killer, the local constable decided to look into the situation. He had Colin tracked down and demanded that he personally give a DNA sample. They had Colin's sample run through the DNA laboratory however back then it took several weeks to get a result. The police were busily working up other leads, when they received word from the laboratory that they had a match between Colin's sample and the victims' vaginal swabs.

With this new revelation the police were ecstatic that now they knew who the suspect was. Then the big question was whether the prosecutors would be able to use the DNA results in a court of law. This one case in Leicester changed the world of criminology forever. No doubt the discovery of fingerprint identification as well as ballistic identification had a significant impact on the advancement of criminology. Nonetheless the advent of DNA individual identification was so revealing that it completely changed the entire approach to homicide investigations.

With this new scientific breakthrough, the next question was what type of acceptance would it receive by the public and the legal world. In England the acceptance of DNA was certainly facilitated by the rage over the killing of the two teenage girls near Leicester. However, the United States prides itself with having all sorts of individual protections that are enumerated in the US Constitution especially the Bill of Rights. The court system is highly protective of the individual's right of privacy.

In the United States there was a reluctance to accept the use of DNA while the rest of the Western world was embracing this new technology. It wasn't until the author, Joseph Wambaugh, wrote the book *The Blooding* did the resistance to DNA start to subside. This one book illustrated the potential DNA had in apprehending criminals. As new protocols were developed it wasn't long before DNA began to be acceptable by the courts.

CHAPTER 29- DNA DATABASE DEBATE

However, the issue of collecting and storing individuals' DNA results has become an extremely controversial topic. Both conservative and liberal groups opposed the creation of a database that would store DNA results for use by law enforcement to help solve future crimes that an individual might commit. Law enforcement wanted to create a giant DNA database which they could use to compare to samples from cold cases as well as future crimes. In that way they could instantly compare a piece of evidence to see if it matched anyone's DNA on file.

Some would like to see every person's DNA in a database. That would certainly make it easier to catch criminals. A side benefit of such an inclusive database would be the deterrent effect it would have on all people. Anyone considering committing a crime would have to think twice since the police would have their DNA on file. Those in favor of a total inclusive system would claim that a law-abiding person in the community would have nothing to fear since if you don't commit crimes you wouldn't be harmed. Nevertheless, there is a large segment of society that is suspicious of government activities.

Law enforcement recognizes that they can't ever have a total inclusion of the population in a DNA database. Yet many people agree that people who have been sentenced to prison should be required to submit a DNA sample. The belief is that when someone has been convicted of a serious crime, they have given up certain rights such as their right to privacy.

Some would agree that a person who has been convicted of a felony offense but not sentenced to prison should also be included in the DNA database. However, many believe that a person convicted of a misdemeanor should not be required to submit a DNA sample for the database.

The most controversial issue has been whether persons who have been merely arrested for a felony charge but not yet convicted should have their DNA results included in a law enforcement database.

Some might say there is nothing wrong with collecting and storing an arrestee's DNA if it might later be used to solve another crime. Isn't it a good thing to solve crime and catch the criminals?

However, some groups fear that the government through law enforcement could or would misuse the DNA database. They claim that the government could use it to keep track of people or discover health issues. The conservative Justice Antonin Scalia stated that collecting and storing DNA results from people who have merely been arrested would be undermining the 4th Amendment's ban of searching a person for evidence of a crime when there is no basis for believing the person was guilty. Justice Goodwin Liu, a liberal on the California Supreme Court, called the storing of an arrestee's DNA in a database a biological dragnet that violated the California Constitution.

The liberal-leaning Los Angeles Times newspaper considers the storing of an arrestee's DNA in a database to be tantamount to law enforcement conducting a genetic fishing expedition.

In response to both the conservative and liberal concerns about arrestees' DNA in the database, law enforcement points out that for years they have collected and retained the fingerprints in a database of people who were merely arrested. No one seems to be outraged by that fact that anyone arrested or taken into custody is automatically fingerprinted and those prints are placed in a fingerprint database called AFIS.

Law enforcement agencies also take booking photos of everyone arrested and store them in a database under the arrestee's name. Those booking photos can be used in photo line-ups involving totally different crimes from the time of the taking of the booking photo.

It wasn't until 2013, that the U. S. Supreme Court upheld a Maryland state law requiring police to collect DNA samples from people who had been arrested and charged with a serious crime. The court said that the DNA results could then be stored in a database and used to solve unrelated crimes. However, there is still a concern that if the arrestee is ultimately cleared of all charges should law enforcement be required to remove that arrestee's DNA results. Some states like California permit an arrestee who has been cleared of the charges to petition the court to order law enforcement to remove that person's DNA results from the database.

CHAPTER 30- USING DNA IN BORIS' TRIAL

Beth understood the DNA result from the ski mask was the crucial piece of evidence in Boris Graham's case. She knew that some jurors might have trouble accepting the DNA results if they had an aversion to science. Beth was well aware that the OJ Simpson trial had cast a negative cloud on DNA. Johnny Cochran built the Simpson case on the fact that LAPD didn't properly collect and preserve the blood from the crime scenes. Further the DNA testing procedures used were not done according to proper standards.

Any time a prosecutor is reliant on DNA evidence, it is like walking through a minefield not knowing what could blow up on you. Would the Defense be attacking the collection process; the storage method; or the procedure that extracted the cellular material from the ski mask? Beth knew she had to be prepared for whatever the Defense wanted to throw at her. During the jury selection Beth had spent considerable time inquiring of each of the potential jurors as to their feelings and acceptance of science. She knew that she couldn't afford to have even one juror who was skeptical of the field of science.

Beth had asked each potential juror as to their feelings about DNA testing. Most jurors indicated they accepted the concept but gave vague answers as to their understanding of DNA. Beth was more interested in the manner in which the potential juror answered the question. Some jurors were hesitant in answering and tried to be noncommittal. Other jurors would indicate they had certain objections to all the new technology and thought it was all confusing.

A prosecutor wants jurors who are open-minded and willing to consider new technology even though they may not be familiar with it. During the jury selection process all prosecutors are looking for any cues that might reveal how a potential juror really thinks about DNA. Every attorney would agree that asking questions during the jury selection process doesn't always guarantee that jurors will reveal their true feelings about science, especially as to DNA testing.

Beth's assessment of the jurors who were selected for this Boris' trial, were that they were willing to listen to the testimony involving the DNA evidence and willing to consider it. None of the jurors seemed to be anti-scientific minded.

During the Opening Statement, Beth had discussed the fact that they the jurors would have to consider DNA evidence testified to by several witnesses. Now it was time for her to call the witnesses to establish that the ski masks were found at the crash site. Next Beth went about establishing the chain of evidence for the ski masks. During Detective Powell's earlier testimony Beth had him explain that he instructed the crime laboratory to determine if there was sufficient cellular material that could be extracted from the ski masks.

Beth's next witness testified to the procedure he used to extract the DNA and how the results were stored and eventually shipped to the CellMark laboratory. The expert witness from CellMark was called who explained the actual analysis of the sample and what the results were. This was the critical part for the prosecution's case. Beth had learned through experience that some of the jurors can become totally lost during the DNA expert's testimony.

Beth kept her questions simple and hoped the DNA expert witness would answer in concise terms not getting lost in the weeds. Beth wanted to develop a comfort level for the jurors. She didn't want the expert witness to sound like a science teacher trying to cover all the details for the final exam. On the other hand, Beth wanted the expert to answer any questions the jurors might have about the procedure used and how the results were obtained. She knew that the Defense attorney would try to create some type of doubt about the procedure used and results that were obtained.

Beth asked the DNA expert what his findings were and the expert stated the following:

The DNA obtained from the sample contained male DNA. The primary DNA profile obtained from the sample matches the DNA profiled obtained from the swab labeled Boris Graham. However, the expert went on to testify: *Michael Parks was excluded as a source of the DNA obtained from the sample. Kirell Taylor was excluded as a primary source of the DNA obtained from the sample but couldn't be included or excluded as a secondary source.*

Then Beth went on to inquire as to what was the likelihood that another human being could have such DNA Profile. The expert said that the approximate frequency in an African American population of DNA profile common to the ski mask and swab labeled Boris Graham was 1 in 27X10 to the 18th power of unrelated individuals.

Beth tried to have the expert explain that the likelihood of someone else in the world having the same DNA was highly unlikely. She knew that the Defense attorney would try to plant the seed that it was possible, although not likely, that another person somewhere in the world at some time in the past or future had the same DNA profile.

After Beth had the expert discuss Boris' DNA results, she shifted to ask him about the tests which were conducted on the other ski mask that contained Kirell's DNA. She didn't spend as much time on Kirell's result since she knew that Boris' Defense attorney wouldn't be interested in creating possible doubt as to Kirell's DNA results.

The DNA expert's testimony was crucial for the prosecution but it was tedious for the jurors to listen to. Yet, it contained so many scientific terms that the jurors had never heard of. When the expert started talking about numbers in the quadrillions it was apparent that some of the jurors had never heard that term used and some didn't even know that was a real number.

Eventually, Beth was finished with the DNA expert and it was then up to the Defense attorney to cross-examine. Boris' attorney went after the CellMark expert witness. It was clear that the Defense attorney had done her homework. She asked certain technical questions which raised a number of issues. After a while some of the jurors seemed to be zoning out on some technical points that she was making. The Defense attorney tried to cast some doubt on the procedure used and the recording of the results.

After a long laborious cross-examination Boris' attorney said, "No more questions for this witness, Your Honor." Beth had to wonder if it was worth asking one more question to clarify a certain point raised by the Defense attorney. Beth could see the pained look on the jurors' faces which seemed to be saying, 'we have heard enough.' In order not to protract the DNA testimony Beth decided enough was enough and said to the judge, "No more questions for this witness, Your Honor." With those words the jurors seemed to feel a sense of relief.

CHAPTER 31- CONSCIOUSNESS OF GUILT

Boris' trial had entered its dull stage. Beth knew the exciting testimony that kept the jurors' attention had come and gone. Now she had to present the evidence regarding **consciousness of guilt** on the part of Boris. The law permits the prosecution to prove that the defendant had done certain acts that could be inferred that he had committed a crime.

Weeks before the start of Boris' trial, Beth had come to your author's office and asked me what would be a way to explain to the jury the fact that the defendant had been on the run for four years. She said that Friday Hanson could establish that Boris and his friend Shake had traveled from Los Angeles to Chicago shortly after the crime. Then Beth indicated to me that Boris returned to Los Angeles for a brief time after which he left for Miami where he remained until he was eventually arrested years later.

I indicated to Beth, she might want to consider using one of the charts I had created for other trials which showed the jury instruction language for 'Flight' which is as follows:

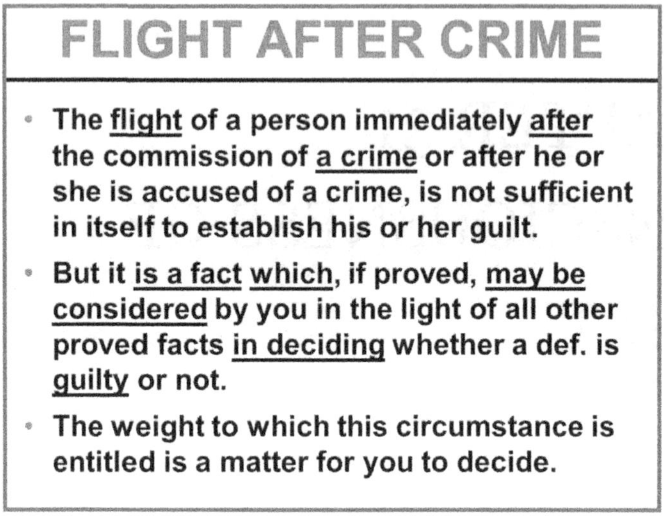

I explained that she could use it in her Argument so that the jurors would know how to apply the legal concept of 'Flight After a Crime.' I showed her the wording that she needed to emphasize which was *"But it is a fact which, if proved (Flight), may be considered by you in the light of all other proved facts in deciding whether the defendant is guilty or not."*

She indicated that she wanted that definition chart added to her Argument slide presentation. But she wanted something more graphic to show the movement of Boris throughout the country. I asked her the various locations Boris had visited. She indicated that she didn't know all the places that Boris had gone but she definitely had witnesses who could testify to him being in Chicago. She went on to say that she had police officers who later saw him back in Los Angeles and this time under a different name. Beth explained that she didn't know when he moved to Miami but she could prove that he was arrested in Miami.

I turned my chair toward my computer and went on the internet and pulled up a map of the USA. I pasted it on a slide and took the arrow tool showing travel from Los Angeles to Chicago and another arrow showing Boris' return to the Los Angeles area. Then I inserted a straight arrow from the West coast to Miami.

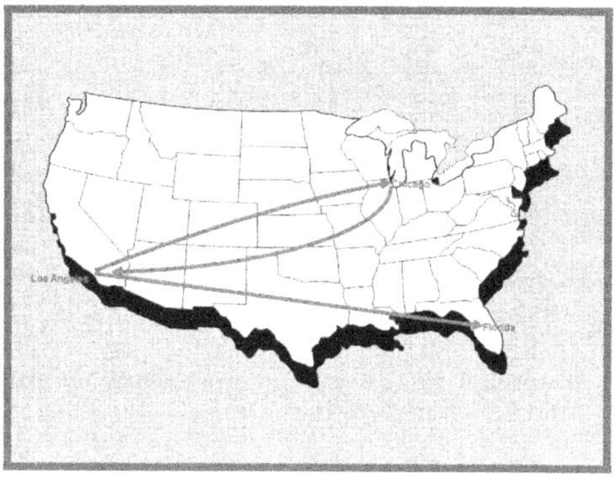

Although the map was very generic, Beth liked it and again said to add it to her Argument slides. Then she asked me what would be a good way to handle the fact that Boris tried to hide his identity. The fact that Detective Powell had seen Boris' photo on the Illinois driver's license showed he had obtained a false identification. In addition, she mentioned that Boris had shown that Illinois driver's license to an LAPD officer during a traffic stop.

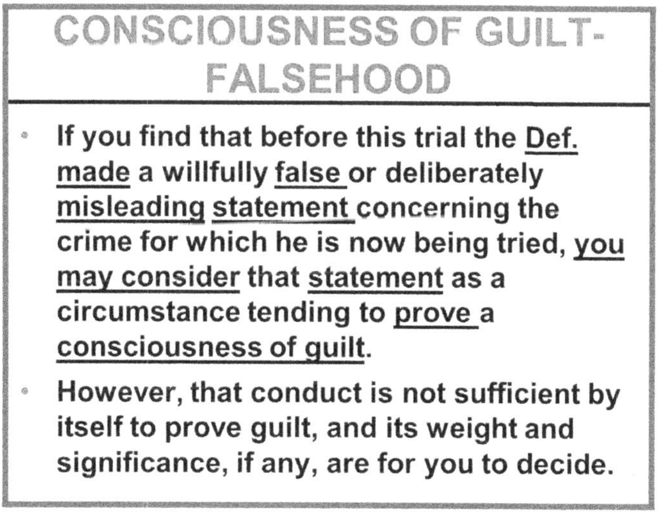

I couldn't quite understand what Beth was explaining to me about the driver's license but I turned to my computer and pulled up the definition of a 'Defendant's Falsehood.' I showed it to her and she nodded and said just add that to the Argument.

The use of evidence regarding 'Flight' and 'Falsehood' by a defendant to prove Conscientiousness of Guilt is of limited usefulness in convicting a defendant. With Beth's vast experience she knew that jurors don't place too much weight on either Flight or Falsehood evidence. Nonetheless Beth was the type of attorney who uses every arrow in her arsenal. To her every piece of evidence might make the difference with some juror. Since she needed a unanimous verdict for a conviction, one can't blame Beth for including everything.

CHAPTER 32- TIME FOR ARGUMENT- UNDERSTANDING THE FACTS

Beth is the type of attorney who seems to do better the more pressure piled on her. Her secret to success is being totally prepared. Granted things can come up out of nowhere at the last minute, but she is good at anticipating all the possible problems in advance. She is ready to handle whatever comes her way By being totally organized her persona radiates confidence in what she is saying to the jurors. That assurance doesn't go unnoticed by the jurors.

When it comes time for the Argument, it is Beth's time to shine. Her mind is working at full speed and her only thought is whether to make last-minute changes to her prepared Argument. When the judge says those magic words, "Does the prosecution wish to make an Argument?" Beth appears to spring out of her chair saying, "Yes, Your Honor." From that moment on, Beth is in total control of the courtroom. The jurors' eyes are fixated on her as they wait to hear what she has to say.

She makes a few congenial remarks thanking the jurors for their attention during the lengthy trial. However, she knows better than to waste any time during the first five minutes of her Argument. Those are considered the Golden Minutes when the jurors are most attentive. Beth immediately started her PowerPoint presentation showing a slide reviewing the facts of the crime. This slide was titled 'SEQUENCE OF EVENTS on February 8, 1999' which allowed her to walk the jurors through the events of that day. She started with the point that Christopher Rawlings called his wife to tell her he would pick up dinner. Then she finished the review by discussing how Kirell Taylor carjacked another car after the crash.

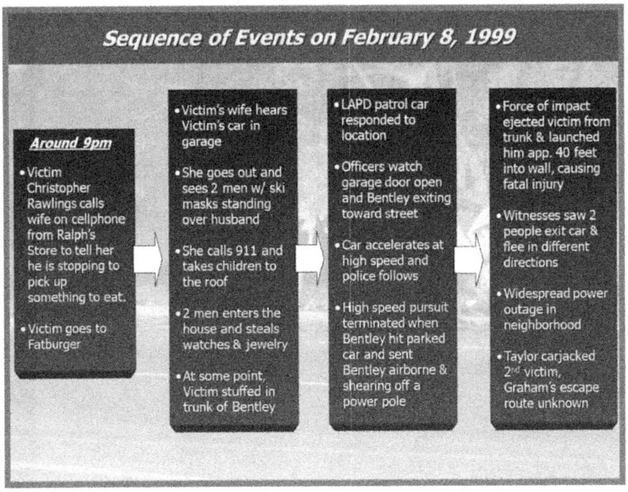

As she was leading the jurors through the facts she could see some of the jurors nodding their heads in agreement. Beth could see that the jurors seemed to be able to grasp what happened that evening of the crime. There wasn't any issue whether there was a residential robbery and the fact that the Bentley was carjacked. The ultimate result was that Christopher was injured and later died.

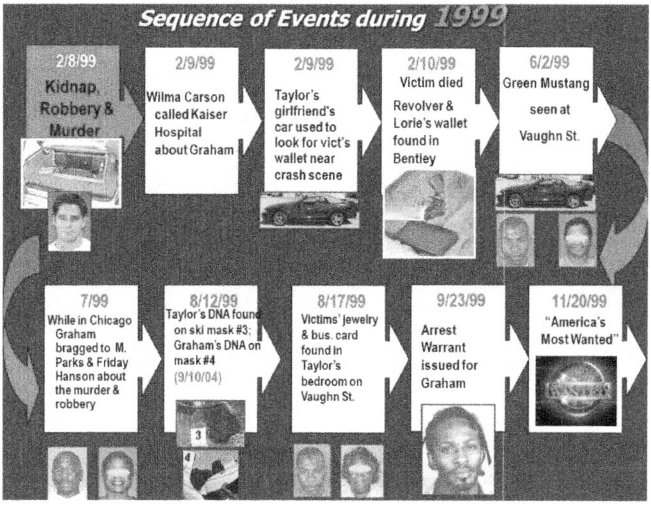

Next Beth wanted to make sure that the jurors had a good understanding when everything happened so she flashed on the screen a slide titled **Sequence of Events during 1999**. Since many of the events occurred over many months, the jurors had to know certain dates because they were like anchors that they would have to rely on.

TIMELINE OF EVENTS

1999	
FEBRUARY 8	Kidnapping and Murder of Christopher Rawlings
FEBRUARY 9	Kaiser Nurse Elizabeth Walker receives Willette Chisolm's inquiry re: Defendant Graham
FEBRUARY 10	Witness D. Colins sees MB at shrubs who left in '97 green Mustang convertible, ID's Dumas & Taylor -Revolver, wallet found in car; Victim dies at hospital
MARCH 12	Takeover Robbery; Taylor's ID, boots, Macys card & Smith's wallet recovered Witness D. Colins ID's Dumas
APRIL 22	Case featured on "America's Most Wanted"
APRIL 23	"America's Most Wanted" segment on Victim's "Presidential" watch
MAY 15	Det. Purdy gets a tip – ran address and found green Mustang convertible with Imani Boujho – Taylor's GF Car registered to Dumas.
AUGUST 12	Taylor's DNA found on ski mask; Graham's DNA found on 2nd mask
AUGUST 16	Tip call re. Graham
AUGUST 17	Taylor calls I/O re: DNA – Search warrant on Irene Betis' house (Taylor's grandmother); Recovered victim's GQ card, Barbie's earrings and bracelet which she ID'd
AUGUST 19	Case filed on Taylor
AUGUST 25	Parks arrested; Bevin Graham tracked down and arrested on a warrant; Def. Graham in car as "Kato", car match in 211
SEPTEMBER 14	Call re: Parks 2nd Call re: Parks
SEPTEMBER 16	Michael Parks interview – *"This is what this is about, that motherfucker Booney!"* pointing to Graham's photo; Park GF Tuesday Henderson interviewed – recovered phony Illinois driver's license with name "Kato Austin" Heard Defendant bragging to Shaq about murder
SEPTEMBER 23	Defendant Boris Graham charged with Christopher Rawling's murder and a warrant issued for his arrest
2004	
JANUARY 13	
JANUARY 28	Bevin Graham and Defendant Boris Graham arrested in Florida

When Beth saw several women writing down the dates, she slowed down her Argument.

The next part of Beth's Argument concentrated on the evidence connecting Boris Graham to the crimes. Beth clicked to her next slide which filled the large courtroom screen and was titled **EVIDENCE PROVING DEFENDANT'S GUILT**.

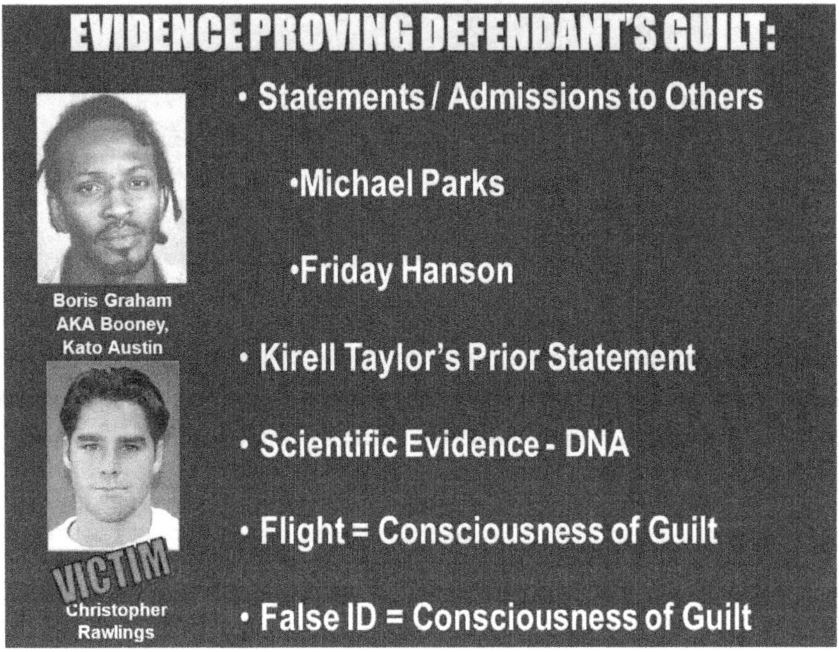

This one slide totally listed the key evidence that proved Boris Graham was one of the robbers/murderers. Beth wanted the jurors to see that the prosecution wasn't relying on just one piece of evidence but several that pointed to Boris' guilt. This slide was merely a springboard she used to show the jurors the details that proved each of those items.

With a click the next slide appeared titled STATEMENTS BY GRAHAM. Beth knew that the jurors most likely had a different understanding as to what an admission was. Generally, it involves a suspect making incriminating admissions to a police officer. She wanted the jurors to understand that the statements that Boris made to his Chicago buddy Michael Parks (Chicken) could be considered as admissions by Boris.

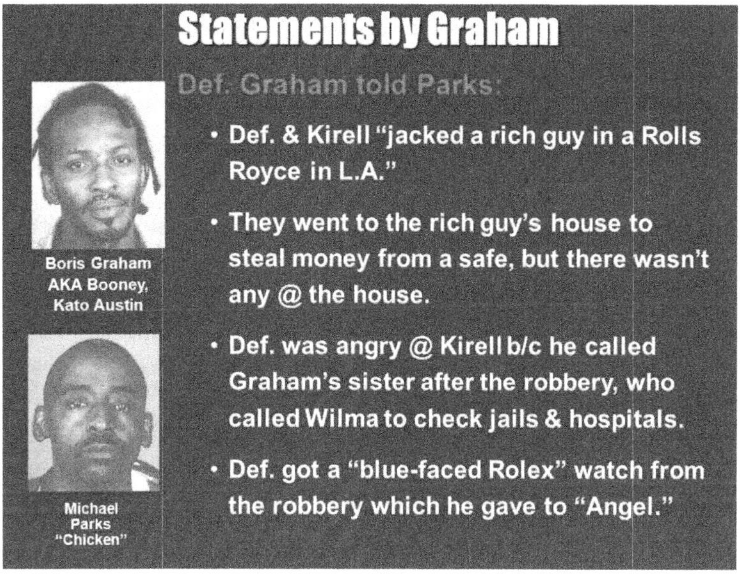

However, this became a convoluted admission since Beth had to use Detective Powell to say what Michael Parks told him what Boris told him. This might seem to be double hearsay but it wasn't. What made it more complicated was the fact that Michael Parks testified in court that he didn't say what Detective Powell said he said. If that isn't bad enough, Parks hadn't permitted Detective Powell to tape record the conversation.

What Beth was asking the jurors to do was to believe that the detective was accurate in his recollection of what Parks had told him. However, on top of that obstacle was the question whether Parks accurately recollected what Boris told him about the robbery and his involvement.

Beth knew that this all required considerable mental gymnastics on the part of the jurors. She knew that the jurors didn't have a warm and fuzzy feeling about

Michael Parks aka 'Chicken.' Most jurors wouldn't give much credence to whatever 'Chicken' said. Yet Beth needed the jurors to believe what Detective Powell claimed Parks told him about Boris' involvement in the Robbery/Murder. Behind Beth on the courtroom screen were the key statements she wanted the jurors to take note of and remember.

First was the outright admission that Boris and Kirell 'jacked a rich guy in a Rolls Royce in L.A.' Next was the statement about the belief the victim had a safe. Also the statement that Boris was mad about Kirell calling Boris' sister about him possibly being injured. Finally, there was the claim that the Rolex watch was given to Angel.

As much as Beth wanted to wash her hands of her witness Michael Parks, she moved on to discuss her next witness Friday Hanson. Even if the jurors didn't like Parks, Miss Hanson was much more likable and she completely corroborated what Parks had told Detective Powell.

Beth's next slide showed the statements that Miss Hanson claimed she overheard Boris tell her boyfriend Parks. The slide spelled out how Boris bragged to Parks about a robbery in L. A. where a rich guy was killed. The slide listed the how the guy fell out of the trunk after a high-speed chase.

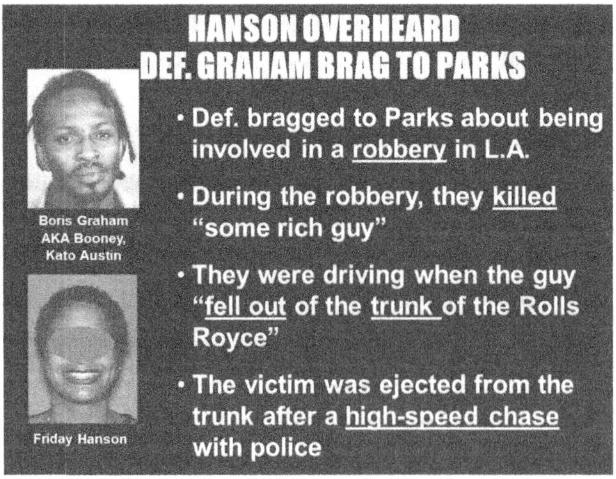

Beth was glad to be finished with the admissions involving Michael Parks. She went on to discuss with the jurors the testimony of Boris' brother's testimony. Robert Graham testified that his brother had said to him that he had planned to rob a white guy at that person's house, but the crime got out of hand and the man was killed in a car crash. He went on to testify that Boris had fled to Chicago to avoid arrest and eventually saw himself on ***America's Most Wanted.***

Beth moved on to Kirell Taylor's highly incriminating statements to Detective Powell when Kirell was in state prison. Even though Kirell testified at the trial that all his prior statements were lies the jurors heard what he had said on the audio tape. Beth knew that the issue wasn't what Kirell had said to Detective Powell but whether she could corroborate what he had said.

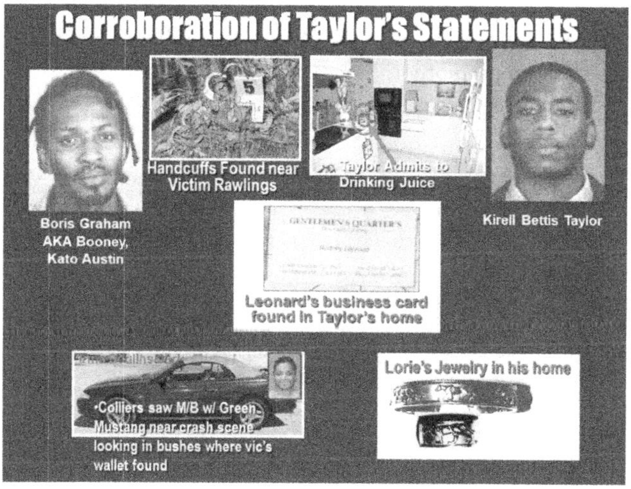

Her next slide was titled Corroboration of Taylor's Statement and appeared on the courtroom screen. The first graphic on that slide showed the handcuffs and the second graphic discussed the orange juice container in the kitchen.

The third graphic showed the green Mustang owned by Kirell's girlfriend that was seen by Miss Colliers the next day when a male black was looking in the bushes where eventually the victim's wallet was found. That was followed by a graphic showing the business card in a Koran in Kirell's bed. Lastly was the graphic of Lorie's jewelry that was found in Kirell's bedroom.

Beth felt that the jurors understood there was more than enough corroboration to support Kirell's statements.

At that point she moved on with her Argument to show the connection between Boris and Kirell. She used a slide to illustrate that both had made statements to the police and others that they were longtime friends. Boris' Defense attorney didn't want the jury to hear about the fact that both Boris, her client, and Kirell were members of the same Pacoima gang. The judge agreed that the issue of gang membership could be prejudicial for the defendant. The judge ordered that neither side should discuss Boris' gang membership in front of the jury.

However, when Beth was arguing to the jury how well the two parties knew each other, she inadvertently mentioned that they had grown up together and shared time together in their neighborhood Pacoima gang. As a matter of fact they both had lived only a block apart from each other.

After Beth had spent considerable time explaining all the statements that incriminated Boris she shifted to the forensic evidence. The jurors may have had doubts about the credibility of some of the witnesses Beth had called to testify. She then proceeded to address the scientific evidence which didn't require the jurors to consider if they believed the witness.

Beth picked up a photo of ski mask item #4 and told the jurors that one item made it perfectly clear who was involved in the robbery/murder of Christopher Rawlings. She pointed to the slide illuminated on the courtroom screen and said these numbers don't lie. She said that the witness from CellMark told the jury with a high degree of certainty that the ski mask #4 contained the DNA of Boris Graham. However, she wanted the jurors to see the exact numbers that the expert from CellMark had relied on. Beth walked the jurors down the various rows showing how the numbers matched up. Beth didn't want the jurors to have to rely on the testimony of the expert witness only. She showed the jurors and they could see with their own eyes that the numbers matched up.

Cellmark Case No.: F991489
Date: 09/10/2004

Item #4 – Ski Mask

Case	F991489 10 ID/ra/ra2	F991489 11 ID	F991489 12 ID	F991489 13 ID
Sample	**Item 99***	**M. Parks**	**Boris Graham**	**Kirell Taylor**
D8S1179	10,12,13,14,15,16	15,17	12,16	12,14
D21S11	29,30,31,31.2	28,35	30,31	29,30
D7S820	9,10,11	10,11	9,11	10,12
CSF1PO	11,12	10	11,[illegible]2	11
D3S1358	13,15,17,18	16,17	[illegible]	13,18
TH01	6,7,8,9,9.3	[illegible]	6,9.3	7,9
D13S317	8,9,11,12,13	[illegible]	8,12	11,13
D16S539	8,9,11,1[illegible]	11,12	9,12	11,12
D2S1338	17,19,23	17,22	17,19	21,25
D19S433	11,13,14,14.2	13,15	14	11,14
vWA	15,16,17	15,20	16	17
TPOX	11	8	11	8,9
D18S51	16,19	14,16	16	12,15
AMEL	X,Y	X,Y	X,Y	X,Y
D5S818	11,12,13	12,13	13	13
FGA	22,24	25,27	22,24	23,24

MATCH

Beth knew that the Defense attorney in her Argument would claim that it wasn't a 100 % match. The Defense would say that it was inaccurate to claim that the DNA found on the ski mask was in fact a match since there was the possibility that someone else could have the same DNA. Beth flipped to her next slide showing the exact wording of the expert's conclusion. She pointed to the wording where the expert had written the frequency of another person having the same DNA as 1 in 27X10 to the 18th power of unrelated individuals.

She explained that the numbers are so unlikely that it was anyone else's DNA. Then Beth had the words 'Matches Defendant' flashed across the slide. That dramatically made it clear in the jurors' minds that the DNA on the ski mask #4 was that of Boris Graham.

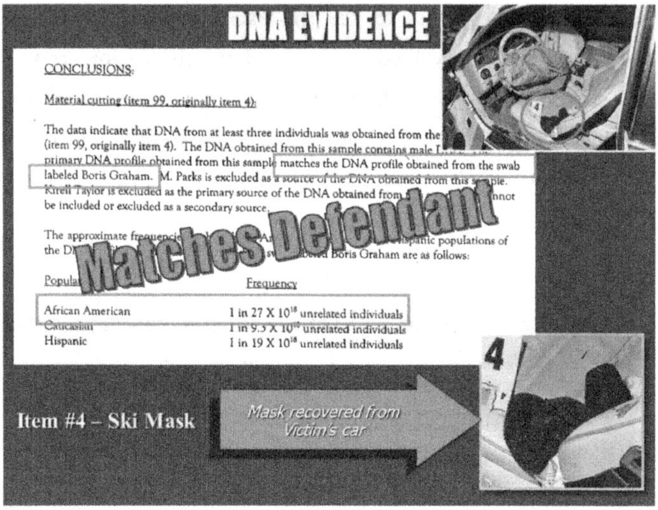

Beth wanted the jurors to comprehend the importance of the DNA evidence connecting the defendant to the crimes. Yet Beth knew that she needed to move on and cover one more point regarding the facts proving guilt. That was when she started discussing Boris' Flight which proved Consciousness of Guilt. Beth showed the map of Boris leaving Los Angeles to go to Illinois and eventually to Florida. She said that was all proved by the testimony of Michael Parks, Friday Hanson and even his brother Robert Graham.

She moved into her next part of the Consciousness of Guilt by showing the false driver's license that Boris had gotten in the name of Kato Austin. Beth knew that this changing of Boris' identification to Austin wasn't sufficient to prove that Boris was involved in the Robbery/Murder of Christopher Rawlings, but she wanted the jurors to have all the evidence to consider during their deliberation.

CHAPTER 33- CULPABILITY OF THE ROBBERS

After briefly discussing the issues showing Consciousness of Guilt, Beth wanted to make a transition in her Argument. She stopped talking and took her written notes and straightened them out. Her eyes were no longer on the jurors but she appeared to be looking over her notes. She picked up several pages and turned them over and placed them in a stack on her left-hand side. She was using these moments as her 'pregnant pause' which effective speakers use to shift topics.

She wanted the jury to digest what she had reviewed with them. She knew that the next part of her Argument was going to be tedious if not boring. Beth needed to keep the jury interested in what she was about to tell them which involved them understanding the law they needed to follow in order to reach verdicts on all the charges.

She shifted her Argument to discussing the issues of Principals and Aiding and Abetting. In this case the jurors would have to decide who was legally responsible for the crimes. Since in this case there were two individuals who were involved, the jury needed to decide to what extent they were guilty of the charges.

Beth started discussing with the jurors the definition of Principal. The reason Beth wanted the jurors to have a firm understanding of the legal concept was due to the fact that it was Kirell who was driving the car which crashed that caused

Christopher's death. Beth didn't want any juror to only find Boris guilty of the robbery but not guilty of the murder since he wasn't driving at the time of the crash.

She explained that a person was a Principal if he were directly involved in the crime or he aided and abetted someone else in committing the crime. She wanted the jurors to understand that either way the defendant was equally guilty.

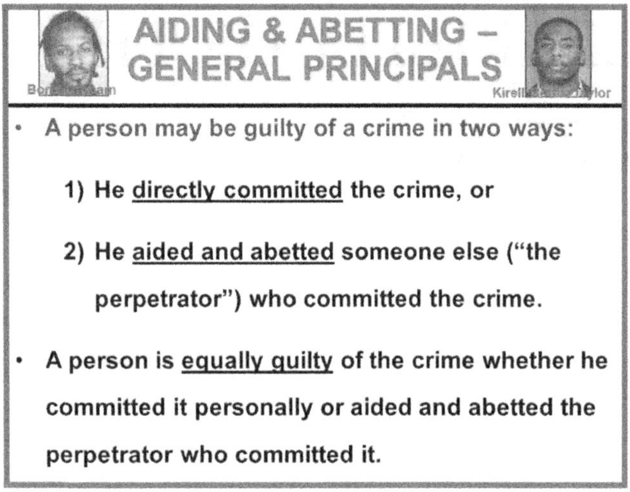

After explaining the legal concept of Principal, she went on to discuss Aiding and Abetting. She wanted the jurors to understand that Boris only had to help the perpetrator on the intended crime which in this case was the Robbery. As long as that was proven then Boris was equally guilty of the Murder.

Beth didn't want to dwell too much on the Aiding and Abetting issue so she used a slide that showed the law on the left side and on the right side she listed the facts the jurors had heard the witnesses testify to. What she really wanted the jurors to remember about the Aiding and Abetting legal concept was that BOTH WERE EQUALLY CULPABLE UNDER THE LAW.

AIDING & ABETTING-INTENDED CRIMES

1. The perpetrator committed the crime,
2. The defendant knew the perpetrator was going to commit the crime,
3. Before or during the crime, the defendant intended to aid & abet the perpetrator in committing the crime, and
4. The defendant's words/conduct did in fact aid, facilitate, promote, encourage, or instigate the perpetrator in committing the crime.

CHAPTER 34- ELEMENTS OF CRIMES

Beth wasn't the type to assume the jurors knew the elements of all the charges against the defendant. It is true that the judge at the end of every trial will read the **LAW** to the jurors. However, anyone who has been a juror in a trial knows how confusing it is to listen to a judge read jury instructions for over a half an hour or longer. First off the instructions are couched in legalese that the average juror has no idea what it means. The court system naively believes that jurors' brains are like a sponge that picks up and retains every word the judge speaks.

Beth doesn't subscribe to this fallacious belief. She knows that jurors need help to decipher what the legal concepts mean. She has slides for each crime that spell out every element the jurors need to consider.

She started out using a slide titled MURDER which laid out the elements for that specific crime. She didn't want the jurors to have the misconception that Murder required the killing to be done with Malice of Aforethought. She wanted to prime the jurors with what is called the Felony Murder Rule.

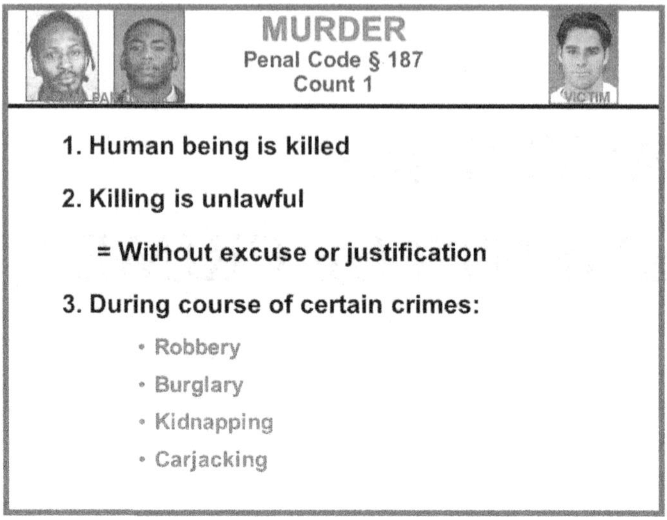

Beth used her next slide to spell out in detail the FIRST DEGREE FELONY-MURDER rule. What Beth continually concentrated on were points number 3 and 4. She knew that the Defense would try to claim that the Robbery was completed when the two suspects backed out of the garage. If that were true the Felony Murder rule wouldn't apply since the suspects didn't cause the death of the victim during the Robbery. She tried to highlight the words that she had at the bottom of the slide stating CONTINUOUS COURSE OF CONDUCT.

FIRST DEGREE FELONY-MURDER
Penal Code §189

1. **The defendant committed a Robbery, Carjacking, Kidnapping &/or Burglary,**
2. **The defendant intended to commit, or aid & abet the perpetrator, in one or more of those crimes,**
3. **While committing those crimes, the defendant or the perpetrator did an act that caused the vic's death,**
4. **There was a logical connection between the act causing the death & the crimes committed.**

= CONTINUOUS COURSE OF CONDUCT

Then she immediately showed the jurors her next slide listing the various forms of CONTINUOUS TRANSACTION. Beth pointed to the factors she had listed on the screen such as:

Fatal act committed to escape after the felony

Fatal act occurred while suspect had control over victim

Fatal act occurred while fleeing the scene of the felony

The Death was a Natural and Probable consequence of the felony.

As complicated as the concept of CONTINUOUS TRANSACTION may seem all the jurors had to find was that at least one of the factors existed and if so then the jurors could move on to the next legal point.

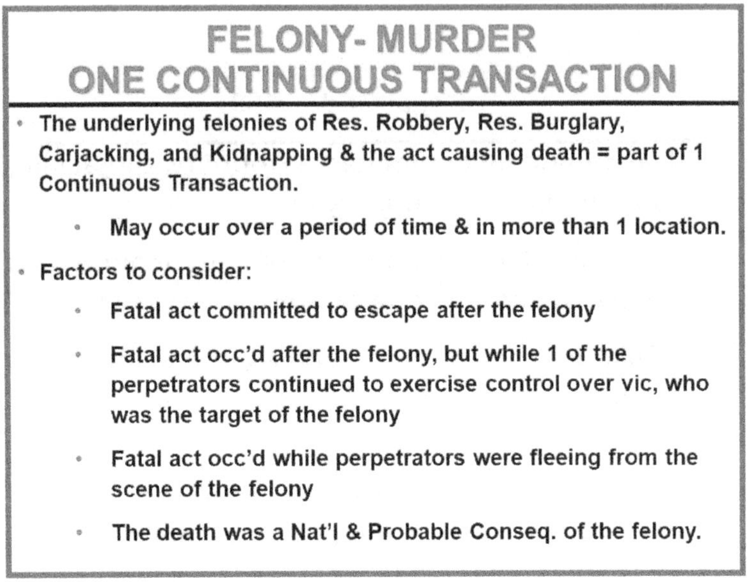

Beth realized that she needed the jurors to use that CONTINUOUS TRANSACTION concept one more time when they had to consider if the Special Circumstance allegation was true. The next slide seemed like a rehash of the same point. Beth explained if they found a Continuous Transaction did exist between the original felony and the death then that Special Circumstances had been proven.

SPECIAL CIRCUMSTANCES:

MURDER IN THE COMMISSION OF A FELONY

Penal Code § 190.2(a)(17)

1. **The defendant committed ROBBERY, CARJACKING, KIDNAPPING, & BURGLARY**
2. **The defendant intended to commit ROBBERY, CARJACKING, KIDNAPPING, & BURGLARY,**
3. **The defendant did an act that caused the death of another person, and**
4. **The act causing the death and the ROBBERY, CARJACKING, KIDNAPPING, & BURGLARY were part of one continuous transaction.**

Beth had finished reviewing the elements of the Murder charge but she still needed to discuss what constituted one of the Underlying Felonies. She would have liked it if the judge had called for a break for the jurors. Yet she knew that everyone wanted this case to be over as soon as possible. She then moved on to the elements of Kidnapping for Robbery.

When she clicked on the next slide it contained lengthy text about Count 2. In order to help the jurors, understand this charge Beth went directly to the real issue which was how far was the victim taken during the kidnapping. Years ago, an appellate court ruled that a victim had to be moved a Substantial Distance. The idea was that if the victim was moved a distance merely incidental to the actual Robbery then that wasn't a sufficient distance for the crime of Kidnapping for Robbery.

Several of the male jurors gave Beth a look as though they couldn't care less how much distance Christopher was driven before he was killed. Beth wanted to make sure that none of the jurors got hung up on the meaning of what was a Substantial Distance.

Then Beth moved on to Count 3 the Residential Robbery. On the big screen Beth listed the elements for that count. She knew that this charge wasn't going to cause any problems for the jurors. The only element that might seem confusing to a juror was element #5 which stated that the defendant intended to permanently deprive the owner of the property. Some juror might think that there was no evidence to show that the suspects might not later return the property to the victim. Beth's explanation was that the robbers took the items and showed no intentions of giving them back.

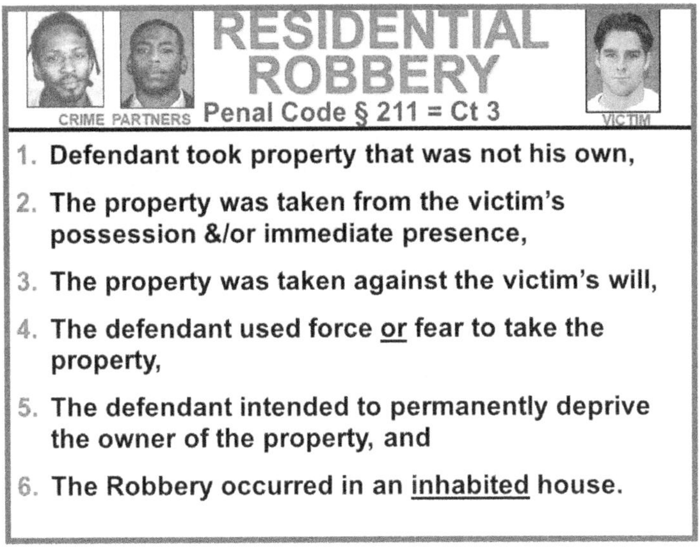

Then Beth flashed onto the screen Count 4 the elements of Residential Burglary. She felt that the elements were self-explanatory and didn't need any discussion. Her only remark was that the word "inhabited" meant being lived in. Beth knew that some people had the false understanding that the crime of Burglary required a "Breaking and entry." She went over the language for Burglary and showed the jurors that there was no requirement that force need to be used to enter the property.

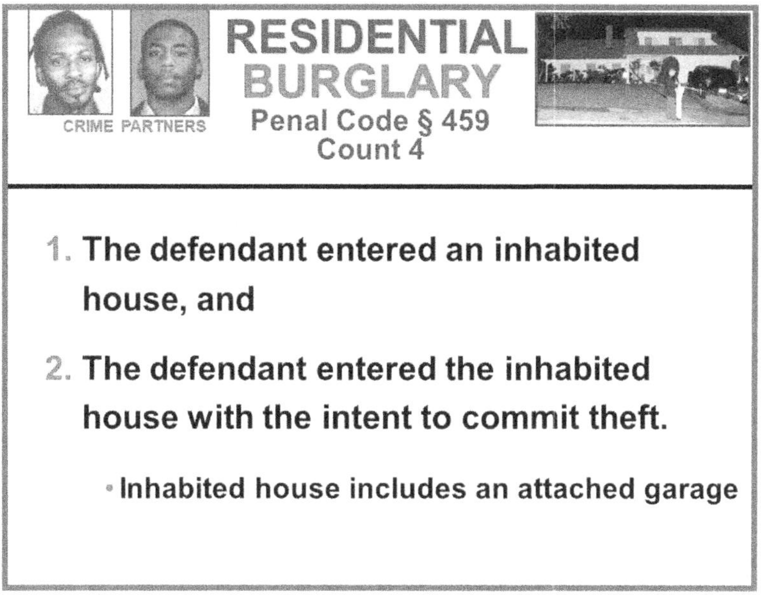

By the time Beth reached Count #5, she had to wonder why the original prosecutor who filed the complaint had listed so many similar charges. This count involved the crime of Kidnapping For Carjacking. Why was this added to the complaint after already having charged Kidnapping For Robbery? Beth realized that she was stuck with the complaint as it was originally charged. When she clicked the next slide showing all six elements for Kidnapping For Carjacking, she hesitated for a moment. True the suspects were guilty of this offense but what was gained by charging it. However, she had no choice but try to explain each element in clear and convincing terms.

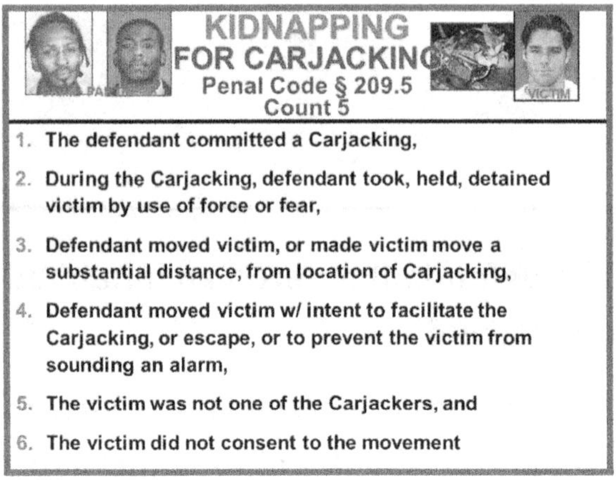

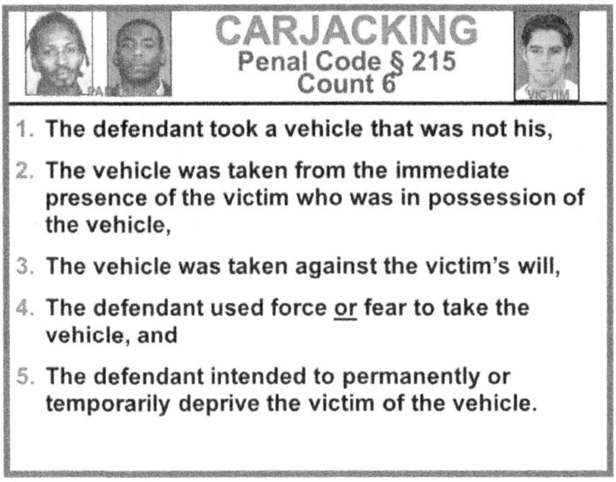

The #6 count was merely the elements for Carjacking which was important since it was one of the Underlining Felonies being used in the Felony Murder rule. She was able to breeze through the Carjacking without much discussion.

Finally, Beth came to the last count which was Evading an Officer Causing Death. This charge seemed anticlimactic in light of the Murder charge. Beth tried to go through the elements which talked about the 'Driver' willfully fleeing from the officers. In this case the prosecution was claiming that this defendant Boris Graham was NOT the Driver. This is where Beth had to refer back to her discussion on Aiding and Abetting. Was she confusing the jurors by asking them to consider whether the driver actually saw the red lights; heard the siren; knew it was a distinctively marked car and that the driver noticed that the officer was wearing a distinctive uniform.

When Beth finished with element #9 she showed on the courtroom screen the slide that she had used in her Opening Statement which showed the map of the pursuit. She pointed to where the pursuit began and showed that the pursuit ended in a crash on Tampa Avenue.

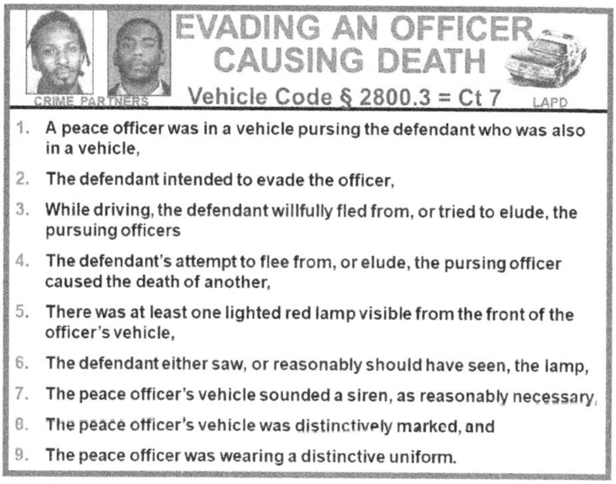

By this time in Beth's Argument the jurors felt they had a crash course in Criminal Law in law school. She knew that she had spent considerable time discussing various points of law. Now she wanted the jurors to put it all in perspective. She clicked on the next slide showing the summary of charges that the jurors would have to render a verdict on.

CHARGES AGAINST DEFENDANT GRAHAM

Cts.	CHARGES	DATE	SPECIAL ALLEGATIONS	VICTIM
1	MURDER PC § 187(A)	2/8/99	• PC 190.2(a)(17) Murder during course of Robbery • PC 190.2(a)(17) Murder during course of Carjacking • PC 190.2(a)(17) Murder during course of Kidnapping • PC 190.2(a)(17) Murder during course of Burglary	CHRISTOPHER RAWLINGS
2	KIDNAPPING TO COMMIT ROBBERY PC § 209(b)(1)	2/8/99	• PC 12022.7(a) Great bodily injury • PC 12022(a)(1) Principal armed with a Firearm	CHRISTOPHER RAWLINGS
3	KIDNAPPING FOR CARJACKING PC § 209.5(a)	2/8/99	• PC 12022.7(a) Great bodily injury • PC 12022(a)(1) Principal armed with a Firearm	CHRISTOPHER RAWLINGS
4	1ST DEGREE RESIDENTIAL ROBBERY PC § 211	2/8/99	• PC 12022.7(a) Great bodily injury • PC 12022(a)(1) Principal armed with a Firearm	CHRISTOPHER RAWLINGS
5	1ST DEGREE RESIDENTIAL BURGLARY PC § 459	2/8/99	• PC 12022.7(a) Great bodily injury • PC 12022(a)(1) Principal armed with a Firearm	CHRISTOPHER RAWLINGS
6	CARJACKING PC § 215(a)	2/8/99	• PC 12022.7(a) Great bodily injury • PC 12022(a)(1) Principal armed with a Firearm	CHRISTOPHER RAWLINGS
7	EVADING AN OFFICER CAUSING DEATH VC § 2800.3	2/8/99	• PC 12022(a)(1) Principal armed with a Firearm	CHRISTOPHER RAWLINGS

This slide was titled CHARGES AGAINST DEFENDANT GRAHAM. It showed in an orderly fashion all of the seven charges from Murder to Evading. Each count had a set of Special Allegations that the jury would have to decide if they applied to that particular count. Beth was hoping whoever was going to be the foreperson, would understand that the jury would have one set of verdict forms for each count. However, on those verdict forms they would have to decide whether the Special Allegation was true or not. As she pointed out in count one, the jury would have to further decide four separate allegations. Beth knew from her years of jury trial experience, often jurors get lost in deciding the special allegation. Occasionally the jury comes back with inconsistent findings which can cause a reversal of the case on appeal. The last thing

Beth didn't want this case to be reversed causing her to have to retry this Graham case.

CHAPTER 35- CONCLUSION OF TRIAL

At this stage of Beth's Argument she could see from the jurors' expressions that some of them had a confused look. Beth knew that discussing the jury instructions with the jurors can be laborious and they can lose their concentration on the key issues in the case. Beth grabbed all her notes and shuffled them back in order and took her Argument folder and slowly closed it.

By doing that she signaled to the jurors that she was ready to present the grand finale. She stepped back and moved to the side of the lectern where nothing stood in her way blocking the jurors. She glanced over to where the defendant was seated next to his Defense attorney and stared at him. After several seconds she clicked to her next slide that showed the Defendant's photo in the center of the slide. Then she started listing the evidence that proved that he was guilty. Each time she clicked an arrow pointed to the defendant listing the incriminating evidence against him. By the time she was finished seven solid arrows surrounded Boris' face.

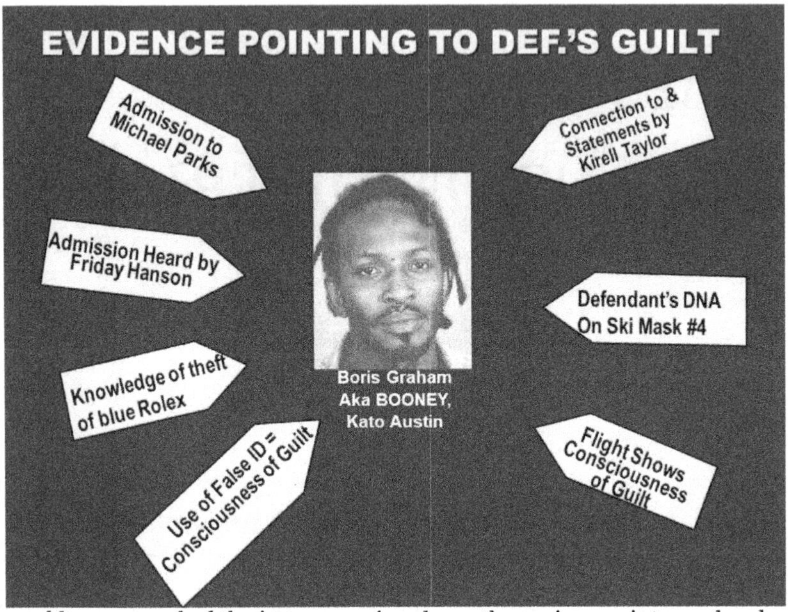

She could see several of the jurors copying down the various points so she slowly picked up her folder with her papers in it and thanked the jury for their attention during her lengthy Argument. She walked over to the counsel table and pulled her chair out and sat down.

Then the judge asked Boris' Defense attorney if she wished to make her Argument. She walked over to the lectern and placed her Argument notes on top of the lectern. She didn't waste any time before attacking the prosecution's witnesses. She went after Kirell Taylor and wondered how anyone could believe anything he said especially a convicted felon. After she cast aspersions on Kirell she started in on Michael Parks. She questioned how do we know what Michael Parks really said? Boris' attorney indicated that the prosecution wanted them to rely on Detective Powell's memory as to what Parks told him over six years ago.

Beth just sat stoically silently at the counsel table as the Defense attorney belittled some of her civilian witnesses. She wanted to shout out the old expression that *you don't find many priests, rabbis or ministers as witnesses in hell*. Then Beth caught herself wondering if that was such a good analogy since so many priests had been involved in child abuse scandals.

Then Boris' attorney went after the ski mask evidence. She indicated that errors could have been made in collecting the cellular material. But her best point was that this was a common ski mask used by many other people in the Pacoima area. Her point was well taken in that there was indication that other people may have used that particular ski mask on other occasions.

Boris' attorney hammered hard on the legal concept of Reasonable Doubt. She spent considerable time raising various doubts. It was going to be the jurors' job to determine if any of those DOUBTS rose to the level of a REASONABLE DOUBT. When Beth was given the opportunity to rebut the Defense attorney's Argument, she addressed the jury by explaining the jury instruction on reasonable doubt.

REASONABLE DOUBT DEFINED

- **It is not a mere possible doubt, because everything relating to human affairs is open to some possible or imaginary doubt.**
- **It is that state of the case which, after the entire comparison and consideration of all the evidence, leaves the minds of the jurors in that condition that they cannot say they feel an abiding conviction of the truth of the charge.**

Beth agreed with Boris' attorney that in this specific case there were certainly some doubts just like in all cases. But she stressed that a Reasonable Doubt was a Doubt in which the jurors cannot say they feel an abiding conviction of the truth of the charges. She reminded the jurors that everything relating to human events are open to some possible doubt but that didn't make it a REASONABLE DOUBT.

CHAPTER 36- CRITIQUE OF THE INVESTIGATION

Sir Arthur Conan Doyle in his series of Sherlock Holmes books would talk about methodically collecting bits and pieces of evidence and later reflecting on which of those items actually led to catching (revealing) the criminal. Needless to say he was working in a make-believe world while real detectives don't have all the time and resources available to investigate a homicide.

Earlier in this book we highlighted various clues in the Rawlings case which a detective like Sherlock Holmes would have considered and reflected upon. Now we want to review those clues to see which ones were productive and which ones were merely a waste of time. The sign of a good detective is one who can spot the clues that have legs and are worth following up on. Also they have to be willing to reject those which may be nothing more than a Red Herring (this term derives from the old custom of using smelly fish to divert hounds from chasing a rabbit).

CLUE # 1 Description of the driver as a male black, 5' 8" to 6' tall, medium build, 20 to 26 years of age wearing a ski mask, burgundy jacket, and dark pants.

USEFULNESS OF CLUE Such a description can be of use when the police officers are searching for a suspect in the immediate area of the crime and shortly after it has occurred. In this case the officer who responded to the crash site could use that information to stop and detain anyone fitting that description. The problem with general physical descriptions is that they lose their usefulness as time goes by. The main value of witnesses who have given a description is to determine if the witness feels that they might be able to identify the suspect from a later photo line-up. That is what the detectives did in this case. When they had a photo of one of the suspects, in this case Kirell Taylor, they contacted those witnesses to see if they could make an identification of him.

As to the description of the wearing apparel it can be useful immediately after the crime but over time suspects change clothes. Most suspects will try to change their appearance by peeling off clothing as they try to escape. In this case one of the suspects did take off his sweat suit which was later recovered. However, that clothing didn't provide any useable evidence.

CLUE # 2 Making plaster casts of shoe prints in the mud of Mr. and Mrs. Lozano's side yard.

USEFULNESS OF CLUE It is easy for a detective to ask the CSI staff to photograph and make plaster casts of the shoe prints. Since it had just rained, the muddy soil was perfect for taking a plaster impression of the shoe prints. In order for such casts to be useful the police have to prove that the shoe prints were of the suspect and not the homeowner or police officers who had tried to chase the suspects. However, the major obstacle of shoe print evidence is that the detectives need to recover the suspect's shoes. When the detectives searched Kirell's bedroom they did find a pair of Nike sports shoes. However, they couldn't be matched to the plaster casts.

There are forensic trace evidence experts who will compare the suspect's shoes with the plaster casts and render an opinion. It is rare that plaster casts are sufficiently detailed to prove beyond a reasonable doubt that the casts were made by the suspect's shoe. Often the shoe prints are used more as cumulative evidence and not the deciding factor as to the guilt of the defendant.

CLUE # 3 The mangled Bentley was taken to a secure tow yard where the CSI team looked for latent prints.

USEFULNESS OF CLUE The detectives requested that the CSI staff attempt to obtain latent prints from the various surfaces in the vehicle's interior and exterior as well as items found in or near the car. Since the detectives found a glove at the crash site, it was unlikely that either suspect left latent prints.

Checking out the Bentley for latent prints was done and numerous prints were found and most belonged to the Rawlings family members and guests who were in the car at various times. The attempt to lift latent prints consumed a great deal of time and resources of the CSI staff. However, it is a standard procedure when conducting an investigation.

CLUE # 4 Taking photos of the muddy shoe prints on the side of the Rawlingses' garage.

USEFULNESS OF CLUE This is similar to Clue #2 but only different in that these prints were at the crime scene of the Rawlings house and could more easily be tied to the robbers. However, the photos of the muddy shoe prints were of no use in the prosecution of defendant Graham. Likewise the plaster casts of these shoe prints didn't result in any evidentiary value.

CLUE # 5 Description of the stolen items such as photos of the jewelry and serial numbers of the Rolex watches.

USEFULNESS OF CLUE The detectives were certain this crime was a planned residential robbery, therefore in the detectives' experience, robbers tend to sell jewelry and watches they obtain during a robbery. In the Rawlings robbery the items taken were of high value which are often quickly sold to 'Fences' (old thieves' slang referring to selling stolen property to someone who will pay only a portion of what the item is worth). In urban areas thieves use pawn shops and swap meets to sell their stolen property.

The detectives needed the photos of the jewelry and serial numbers of the Rolex watches in order to provide a description which the police pawn shop detail could use when checking out the pawn shops.

In this Rawlings case the detectives were able to recover several of the stolen items in defendant Kirell's bedroom. The detectives had received photos of the jewelry from Lorie which they used to be able to identify the stolen items of jewelry. The finding of the jewelry in Kirell's bedroom, turned out to be one of the strongest pieces of incriminating evidence against Kirell.

CLUE # 6 Local hospitals were contacted regarding a possible injured person being admitted as a result of a traffic accident. At 12:30 a.m. Elizabeth Williams from the local Kaiser Permanente Hospital received a call from a person who gave the name of Wilma. This individual asked if a Boris Graham or Jubba Pattis had been admitted to the hospital due to some type of traffic accident. Ms. Williams didn't have any such patient at their hospital but later she ran the name through the hospital's prior patient files. She noticed that Boris Graham had been a previous patient. She contacted the police and provided them that information.

USEFULNESS OF CLUE When the LAPD detectives received that information, they reviewed it and followed up with tracking down the person named Wilma. That person turned out to be a Wilma Carson who admitted making the inquiry at the local hospital. However, the detectives weren't able to track down this Boris Graham and merely placed a note in their files about the inquiry.

Ultimately this became an important fact however Wilma's information she had received was hearsay and couldn't be used to prove Boris' connection to the crash site.

Without a doubt someone at LAPD should be given credit for being insightful enough to think about contacting all the local hospitals asking them to be on the lookout for injured parties from a traffic accident. Granted some people might believe that it was improper for LAPD to make such a request since this is a form of invading an injured person's right to privacy. Their thinking is that the police should not do anything that will discourage an injured person from seeking treatment at a hospital. Furthermore, others might say that LAPD's action was racist since they gave the description that the suspects running from the crash site appeared to be male African Americans.

Most likely Sherlock Holmes would have been impressed by how insightful the police were. You almost can hear Holmes boasting to his colleague, "My Dear Watson that was nothing but superb police work."

CLUE # 7 Jack Mayes on Oxnard Street contacted the police about finding a pile of clothes between two parked cars.

USEFULNESS OF CLUE The detective who received that information had to think in his own mind as to whether those clothes could be relevant to the identity of the parties who escaped from the Bentley. The detective couldn't assess how useful the clothes were until he could personally observe them. The clothing could have been items dropped from someone's laundry or just a homeless person discarding old clothing.

In an abundance of caution, the detective made arrangements to meet Mr. Mayes where he had found the clothes. The detective looked at the sweat suit and when he found no identification, he reached into the pockets to see if anything could be found showing who had possessed such a sweat suit. No papers or any form of identification could be found.

The detective did collect the clothing as possible evidence but the detectives weren't ever able to prove who they belong to. In other words, this clothing proved to be of no value in either trial.

CLUE # 8 Donna Colliers who resided on Tampa Avenue saw a person looking for something in the bushes next to the street. She contacted the police on what she had observed. She provided a description of the person as a male black clean-shaven, close-cropped hair, around 6' tall and somewhere between 25 to 30 years of age, with a medium build.

USEFULNESS OF CLUE When detective Powell received this information, he couldn't determine whether this was just a wild goose chase. Sometimes a detective takes a deep breath and says okay let me see if this clue will grow into something. Since this sighting occurred on the next day, it was questionable as to its relevancy. But there was that long shot that somehow it was connected to the fleeing robbers. Detective Weston was assigned to meet with Miss Colliers and listened to her describe this man who had a frantic look on his face as he paced back and forth in the landscaping next to the street.

This witness emphasized how the actions seemed suspicious since the person had left the car parked in the right-hand lane of traffic. She pointed out the site where the man was looking in the bushes. Detective Weston walked into the landscaped area not knowing what he was looking for but he was desperate for any viable clue.

He knew that he shouldn't be wasting time during the golden 48 hours of any homicide investigation. As Weston maneuvered around the various shrubs, he could see trash in the form of beer cans and empty cigarette packs. Since it had recently rained the detective had to do some tricky footwork to avoid the mud puddles. Several times he had to lean down to get a better view of what was actually scattered on the ground. Miss Colliers continued to shout instructions to Detective Weston as to where she had seen the man rummaging around.

Weston had to wonder why was he wandering through all this brush when he noticed something that looked like a leather item caked in muddy debris. He leaned over and could see it was a wallet. At that emotional moment the detective wanted to pick up the wallet to see if there was any identification in it. However, as a homicide investigator he had to put the brakes on his emotions in order not to destroy possible latent prints or DNA on the wallet. With a pen he was able to flip the wallet open and there were several credit cards with the name Christopher Rawlings printed on them.

Detective Weston was elated that they had stumbled across the victim's wallet where it appeared that one of the robbers had been looking for it. The detective had to step back and assess what he had just uncovered. His first thought was whether Miss Colliers could later identify the person she had seen. As you the reader have learned Miss Colliers was shown photo line-ups and was unable to identify Kirell or Boris. As a matter of fact, she identified someone who had nothing to do with this case.

In the end Miss Colliers wasn't going to be useful as an eyewitness but she was able to provide information about a vehicle which would become crucial to the case.

CLUE # 9 Donna Colliers described the car as a tan-over-green convertible sports car like a Mustang.

USEFULNESS OF CLUE It was Miss Colliers' description of the Mustang vehicle that became a pivotal point to the case. The detective asked her if she should see a similar car for her to give them a call. The likelihood that a civilian would go to that much trouble was highly unlikely. Nevertheless, Miss Colliers contacted the police and provided them with information that a similar car was parked at one of the shopping centers in the San Fernando Valley. She gave them the license plate number and the police were able to obtain a very good reliable description of the Mustang. Granted at that point, they only knew that type of Mustang was used in the search for the wallet on the next day. No one was able to connect the car to the actual residential robbery of the Rawlings house.

As you the reader have already learned that when the detectives were checking out Kirell's residence, they saw a similar Mustang parked in front of the house. The detectives wrote down the license plate number and later it was learned the vehicle was registered to Irma Boulins who was Kirell's girlfriend. This became one of the major breakthroughs in the case against Kirell.

This clue started out as a civilian being suspicious of someone looking through the bushes the day after the Bentley crash. The willingness of the civilian to take notice of this and contact the police was remarkable.

CLUE # 10 Neighbors who saw a person running away from the crash site described him as a male black, between 20 and 30 who was of medium size and weight wearing dark clothes.

USEFULNESS OF CLUE Again these descriptions by the neighbors who got a glimpse of a person running through their yards were something that could be useful when the detectives had names of possible suspects. This clue was useful in giving the detectives a list of possible eyewitnesses but the descriptions were so generic as to be of limited value.

CLUE # 11 The detectives started showing a photo lineup which included a photo of Boris Graham.

USEFULNESS OF CLUE Early in the investigation the detective had received the name of Boris Graham in regard to someone making an inquiry about him at a local hospital. With that name the detectives prepared a photo line-up which they showed to various people who claimed to see a person running from the crash site. However no one was able to positively identify Boris as one of the parties running away. Most likely the witnesses hadn't seen Boris but more likely saw Kirell trying to get away. At that point in the investigation, Kirell's name had not surfaced as a suspect therefore the witnesses weren't shown a photo line-up of Kirell.

CLUE # 12 Leonard Shidler was in custody for a burglary case and acted as an informant. He indicated that the brains behind the killing was a Ken Kaplan who was an associate of Christopher Rawlings. He further explained that one of the robbers was a Donald Tran.

USEFULNESS OF CLUE In many homicide investigations the detectives are given the name of a possible suspect by an informant. It may seem like a gift that homicide detectives dream of. However, the seasoned homicide detectives are more than cautious when such an offer is extended to them. What old timers have learned is that it may turn out to be a 'wolf in sheep's clothing' (This refers to a person who appears to be friendly or helpful but who really is dangerous or dishonest. The derivation of this saying is from Matthew 7:15 referring to the Sermon on the Mount when Jesus spoke of false prophets in sheep's clothing but inwardly, they are ravening wolves.)

The LAPD detectives liked the idea of having a named suspect but they could see from the manner in which the residential robbery was conducted it didn't fit what the informant was telling them. The detectives contacted the victim's brother and asked if he was aware of any of the named individuals. The brother said he was very close to Christopher and he never had spoken about any of the people mentioned by that informant.

Fortunately, the detectives didn't become distracted by this informant's revelation. They checked it out and moved on to the clues that had possibilities.

CLUE # 13 January 31, 1999, Daniel Berg was a victim of a residential robbery by two masked men in which the victim was struck in the face. The items taken were a Rolex watch and several television sets. This crime occurred three miles east of the Rawlings house.

USEFULNESS OF CLUE The facts of this Berg residential robbery were definitely similar and the detectives wanted to compare notes. During this time period the San Fernando Valley was having an outbreak of residential robberies since they were easy to pull off and the rewards were lucrative. The communities of Woodland Hills, Encino and Sherman Oaks were known as affluent areas where robbers could easily spot the so-called 'high rollers.' As soon as a potential victim was spotted all the robbers had to do was follow that person home and pull off the robbery.

The robbers wore ski masks and gloves and the victims were never able to identify the robbers. Detective Powell recognized that the detectives in the Berg robbery had no viable suspects to investigate. Powell indicated that if the Berg detectives came up with any suspects to let him know and he would do likewise for them.

CLUE # 14 An orange-juice container was recovered from the Rawlingses' kitchen table which one of the suspects had drunk from. The hope was that there might be latent prints on the container and possibly some bodily fluids which could be analyzed for DNA.

USEFULNESS OF CLUE This was a long shot. First the orange juice container had condensation on the outside of the container. The chances of lifting prints were remote but at the early stages of a homicide investigation there is a tendency to collect everything in sight. But with subsequent reflection it became obvious this orange juice container wasn't going to yield any useful results.

CLUE # 15 The police recovered from the ground next to the open driver's door a police scanner.

USEFULNESS OF CLUE What was the likelihood that the police could trace the recovered scanner back to the person who had purchased it? You the reader already know that the detectives spent considerable investigative time checking with the manufacturer and tried to trace where the various scanners were sold. The best the detectives came up with was that several companies sold the scanners in the Los Angeles area. None of the companies kept records of the serial numbers when they sold the scanners to the public. Tracing the ownership of the scanner may be considered a waste of time. However, Homicide Detectives learn that sometimes it is the long shots that pay off the most.

CLUE # 16 The police recovered a pair of handcuffs at the crash site near a cinder block wall.

USEFULNESS OF CLUE Tracing back the ownership of the handcuffs most likely was just as much a long shot as tracing the scanner. The best the detectives came up with was that this type of handcuff was used by security guards. Some handcuffs may have serial numbers but seldom do the sellers keep track of who the handcuffs are sold to. In retrospect, this may have been a waste of time trying to track down the owner of the handcuffs.

CLUE # 17 The detectives recovered a revolver on the floor mat of the Bentley.

USEFULNESS OF CLUE Since the scanner and handcuffs couldn't be connected to any suspect, the gun found on the floorboard had real potential of revealing who was its owner or user. The gun had a serial number which was traced to an elderly gentleman. The detectives were thrilled that they had a name that could be investigated. You as readers are aware that there was a family dispute as to who was given or had taken the gun. Even though the detectives knew who the two parties were they couldn't prove who might have sold the gun to gang members. The other possibility was that the gun could have been stolen from the old man when he was ill.

The bottom line was that the gun had been one of the most promising pieces of evidence, but it turned out to be a big nothing and unfortunately had used up considerable investigation time.

CLUE # 18 Two ski masks were found near the open driver's door of the Bentley. They didn't have serial numbers or any way to know who purchased them. Could either ski mask contain something that would indicate who used it?

USEFULNESS OF CLUE When the detectives saw the two ski masks the initial reaction was that this was going to be a very difficult case to solve since there wouldn't be any eyewitnesses who could identify the robbers. The fact that there were ski masks found next to the Bentley was a giant negative for the detectives. It wasn't until all the viable pieces of evidence proved to be worthless, that the detectives started to reconsider the value of the ski masks.

As you the readers have been told it was like a last-ditch effort by Detective Powell. He had the ski masks examined by the SID lab to see if there was sufficient amount of dry saliva around the mouth holes. To the detectives surprise the lab was able to obtain a sufficient amount of cellular material to have analyzed for a suspect's DNA.

It turns out that each of the ski masks contained the DNA of one of the suspects. This placed both defendants in the position that they would have to testify in front of the jury to explain why their DNA was found on the ski masks. True the defendants could claim that these ski masks were used by their local gang and at one time they may have used one of the ski masks during gang activities. This put the defendants on the defensive and they would have to be very convincing to the jury.

In both trials the ski-mask DNA evidence became the crucial link to convict both of them for the crimes they committed.

CLUE # 19 The police recovered a remote control of a garage door opener. On the front of it was a blood smear.

USEFULNESS OF CLUE When the detectives originally saw the remote-control, they had the hope that the biological blood or bodily fluid on it could be connected to the defendants. When the DNA analysis came back it proved that the blood smear on the item was from the victim Christopher Rawlings. This proved to be a useless clue.

CLUE# 20 Mrs. Vargas was carjacked by a black male shortly after the car crash near Tampa Avenue. When she was thrown out of her car, her purse remained and it contained her credit and debit cards. When she recovered her car her purse and contents were missing. On February 9, 1999, her debit card was used at a Chevron service station in South Los Angeles.

USEFULNESS OF CLUE Detective Gaines contacted the Chevron service station and learned that there were no security cameras that showed the office or the area of the gas pumps. Because this was a busy service station no one could remember who used the debit card. This had been a long shot which consumed valuable time and provided no identification of the user of the debit card.

CLUE # 21 The TV program *America's Most Wanted* aired on April 3, 1999, with a segment relating to the Rawlings case. A month later on May 19, 1999, the lead detective received on his voice mail a message telling them who they should be looking for.

USEFULNESS OF CLUE This TV program has been a godsend to many homicide detectives. The concept for such a TV show originated in Germany and later in Britain but didn't get started in the United States until 1987. In that year, Fox executives Stephen Chao and Michael Linder decided to produce a similar program titled America's Most Wanted. Initially, there was a frantic search for a host for the new program. Former police officer and author, Joseph Wambaugh, was contacted but he wasn't interested because he didn't believe that a national dragnet would work in the States. Next they contacted Rudolph Giuliani the former U.S. Attorney from New York who refused the offer since he had other ambitions he wished to pursue. Other names suggested were Bob Woodward and even victims advocate Theresa Saldana.

Finally, Fox offered the hosting job to John Walsh who had gained publicity after his six-year-old son was kidnapped and murdered in 1981. He agreed to host the pilot program that aired on February 7, 1988, which highlighted David James Roberts an escapee who had been convicted of a brutal murder. Within four days of that broadcast he was captured as a direct result of airing that pilot program. This demonstrated how effective such a program could be in capturing bad guys. Soon those in law enforcement who were skeptical of such a program recognized the value of such a TV series.

The show's purpose was to profile and assist law enforcement in the apprehension of fugitives wanted for murder, rape, kidnapping, child molestation and other serious crimes. To the credit of this TV series there were 1,202 people who have been captured as a direct result of airing an episode about that particular suspect. *America's Most Wanted* became a major hit for Fox TV and after 23 years went on to be the longest-running program for Fox until its final episode was aired on June 18, 2011.

When *America's Most Wanted* did an episode on the Christopher Rawlings case they didn't know who the real suspects were. Within weeks of the airing of the Rawlings episode one of the detectives on the case received a phone message on his voice mail telling him he should be looking for a person named "Key-Rail" on Vaughn Street in Pacoima. That was the crucial key to unlock this case and led to the arrest and conviction of Kirell Taylor.

However, in this Rawlings case the TV series *America's Most Wanted* played a dual role. In 2004 another episode was broadcasted and this time the detectives were specifically looking for Boris Graham. Although Boris had been successful in eluding the police, it was that TV program that revealed he had been hiding in Florida where he was arrested.

Without a doubt this TV series has played a significant role in solving cases as well as allowing law enforcement to locate fugitives. It was a double hit in the Rawlings case.

CLUE # 22 When detectives drove to the Vaughn Street address, they noticed a tan-over-green Mustang parked in front. This description of the Mustang was the same as given by Donna Colliers as to the car in the street where someone was looking for something in the bushes.

USEFULNESS OF CLUE We have previously discussed the importance of the green Mustang convertible. The detectives were astute enough to recognize that this particular vehicle fit the description that Miss Colliers had given. By writing down the license plate number and checking it through DMV, the detectives then had the name of one of the suspect's girlfriends and knew her address. This clue provided the detectives with vital information they used to track down defendant Kirell.

CLUE # 23 The detectives received information that on March 12, 1999, a car agency on Prairie Avenue in Hawthorne had been robbed. One of the robbers Eric Sterling attempted to escape in a Dodge Intrepid taken from the car agency. The next day the police located the Dodge Intrepid abandoned. When they conducted a search of the Dodge, they found in the trunk a wallet hidden in a pair of boots. When they examined the wallet, it contained the identification of Kirell Taylor.

USEFULNESS OF CLUE This clue was a long shot. The detectives had a strong suspicion that Kirell was involved in the Rawlings case but there wasn't sufficient evidence that could be used in court against him. There was no way of knowing how

Kirell's wallet ended up in the trunk of a car used in a robbery. The Hawthorne detective had a crime but connecting Kirell to it was tangential. The facts of the Hawthorne case were totally different from the Rawlings residential robbery. It involved a takeover of a car agency in Hawthorne which was 20 miles from the San Fernando Valley where Kirell hung out.

Although this clue might be considered a waste of time, this clue permitted the LAPD detectives to have contact with Kirell's parole officer. This led to the next clue which paid off.

CLUE # 24 Kirell was asked to meet with his parole agent and required to provide a blood sample. The LAPD detective obtained that blood sample.

USEFULNESS OF CLUE The detectives had received word that the Crime Lab had been able to extract sufficient cellular material from the ski mask. This meant that the detectives needed to learn Kirell's DNA. Since Kirell's DNA wasn't in any database the detectives needed to find a way to obtain Kirell's DNA. The LAPD detectives worked with the Hawthorne detectives to contact Kirell's parole officer.

When Kirell came into the parole office he was met by his parole agent and the detectives from both LAPD and Hawthorne PD. After a heated discussion Kirell submitted to his blood being taken by a nurse. This blood sample was ultimately given to the LAPD detectives who had it sent to CellMark Lab to determine its DNA. When that was compared to the DNA from one of the ski masks it was a statistical match.

CLUE # 25 Two pieces of stolen jewelry were found in a little basket in Kirell's bedroom.

USEFULNESS OF CLUE Fortunately the detectives conducted a thorough search of Kirell's bedroom. Since Lorie had given photos of the bracelet and earrings which were stolen, detective Powell could see that the jewelry found in Kirell's bedroom matched the photos of the jewelry. True the jewelry didn't have serial numbers to identify it, however with the photos even the jurors could see how similar these items were.

CLUE # 26 A business card of Rodney Leonard for Gentleman's Quarters was found in a Koran at the base of Kirell's bed.

USEFULNESS OF CLUE If the jewelry wasn't enough, finding the business card in a Koran at the foot of Kirell's bed may have been the clincher. Granted Mr. Leonard had given out his business cards to many potential customers, however, he remembered giving it out to a black male who was asking about the price of the suits. Also, the Woodland Hills store was many miles from the Pacoima area where Kirell lived and hung out.

CLUE # 27 Detectives learned that Kirell's girlfriend was Irma Boujourx and she lived on Via Verde Street in Palmdale and at one time Kirell had lived with her. Later the detectives obtained a search warrant for her place and car.

USEFULNESS OF CLUE By the time the detectives conducted the search of Boujourx's place in Palmdale, the detectives had made their case on Kirell. When they searched the trunk of her car they found a citation made out to Kirell Taylor. There also were numerous documents which appeared to be used to make fraudulent identifications.

CLUE # 28 On the next day August 8, 1999, the detectives felt they had enough evidence to sit down with defendant, Kirell Taylor, and get his side of the story. They met him at the Central County Jail and advised him of his Miranda Rights. He waived his rights and was willing to talk to the detectives. But when they started asking questions about the Rawlings case, it was like hitting a stone wall. Kirell shook his head and said that he had not been involved in that crime nor had he ever been in that Bentley that crashed. At that point he refused to talk without having an attorney present.

USEFULNESS OF CLUE The detectives would have liked to have obtained statements from Kirell either as a confession or as to admissions to his involvement in the crime. Back in 1999, LAPD detectives were trained in the Reid approach as to conducting interrogations. However, as the years have gone by there are newer techniques developed to encourage suspects to waive their Miranda rights and continue to talk to the detectives.

The Reid method was outlined in a book in 1962, titled ***Criminal Interrogation and Confessions*** which spelled out how detectives should approach interviewing a suspect. An interrogation should be designed to persuade a suspect that confessing is the only sensible option. The Reid method of interviewing usually took place in a small claustrophobic interrogation room in which the detective has a theme that the subject is guilty. The detective explains that they have incontrovertible evidence of the person's guilt or even claim to have facts which don't even exist. Also, the detective can try to minimize the crime in a consoling way to make the subject think he was justified in committing the crime.

The Reid interrogation technique indicated that detectives should look for physical behavior such as fidgeting or breaking eye contact. It was believed that such acts were a sign of being deceptive. Later scientific studies showed that there was no reliable way to detect truthfulness by observing a person's physical actions.

However, early in 1990, DNA evidence became more readily available to law enforcement. By that time, evidenced was building that certain defendants who were convicted and sentenced to prison were being exonerated of the crime by DNA results. About a third of the wrongfully convicted had confessed to the crimes. Those confessions had been obtained by using the Reid approach and the goal was to make the subject want to confess in order to end the interrogation.

It wasn't until 2010, that the government was concerned with the reliability of information that was obtained by torture in U.S terror investigations. That was when the government formed the High-Value Detainee, Interrogation Group (HIG) which was a joint effort of the FBI, the CIA, and the Pentagon. In place of waterboarding and coercion the new HIG technique was created to conduct noncoercive interrogations.

The HIG interrogation technique was expanded in other countries like England and Canada and is used by their law enforcement agencies when conducting interrogations. The old Reid interrogation method was replaced with a more non-accusatorial approach and it emphasized 'rapport-building.' It wasn't until 2012, that LAPD actually took a look at the HIG interrogation tactic. LAPD sent several of their Robbery Homicide Division detectives to Washington DC for HIG training.

They decided to utilize the HIG technique and to establish a non-accusatorial setting by getting away from the confining interrogation rooms. The detectives try not to be threatening but appear to be interested in the subject's understanding of the facts. The goal of the interview is to get the subject talking and keep him or her talking as long as possible. The objective is not to be confrontational or attempt to extract a confession from the subject, but only interested in obtaining as much information as possible.

The net result is that the subject makes so many statements that some end up being admissions or become inconsistent statements. Also this technique requires hours of preparation time to understand all the facts so the detectives know what areas to go into and areas to avoid. The key to this approach is to be non-combative and try to gain the subject's trust to keep him talking. If he is guilty, he will eventually make some type of admission.

In this Rawlings case which occurred in 1999, the detectives had never heard of the HIG interrogation method. Possibly if they had used it on Kirell he might have continued to talk to them and in the process make some type of admissions that could have been used against him.

As to Boris Graham he was arrested in 2004, still before the HIG approach was introduced to LAPD. Since Boris had over five years to think about his story, he most likely would not have been a good candidate for the HIG technique. However, what was amazing was the very astute interrogation of Michal Parks conducted by Detective Powell back in the Cook County Jail. He used many of the HIG techniques by trying to get Parks to continue to talk. The result was that Powell was able to eliminate Parks as a suspect and ended up making him a witness for the prosecution.

The interview of Kirell Taylor in state prison in 2006 was so well done that Kirell turned into a witness for the prosecution which was used to convict his partner in crime. Detective Powell let Kirell talk and talk which seemed to be from the HIG playbook even though this technique hadn't been created. Maybe Detective Powell was slightly ahead of his time.

CHAPTER 37- EPILOGUE

After the final jury instruction was read, the jury filed out of the courtroom and into the jury deliberation room. There was a sigh of relief that the three-week trial was over. The courtroom clerk asked Beth and Boris' attorney what phone number they could be reached at for the remainder of the day just in case the jurors had a question. No one expected a quick verdict with all the charges and all the special allegations that needed to be decided.

BETH SILVERMAN

Beth went back to her temporary DA office in the courthouse anticipating a long wait. She wanted to unwind after the intense Argument. She personally puts her heart and soul into every trial. Her brain was still stuck in full throttle and her mind replayed every facet of her Argument. She mused to herself on what she should have done or how she should have emphasized one issue or another. Then an inner voice told her to "shut up" that it was over and there was nothing she could do now since it was in the hands of the jurors.

She snapped out of blaming herself for not arguing certain points. But then her mind started rethinking the wisdom of accepting the present set of jurors. She began having second thoughts about some of the jurors she had left on the jury. She knew she didn't have a perfect set of jurors since she had to accept several questionable jurors in order to get the Defense attorney from objecting to her strong jurors. She knew all too well that the jury selection process is a 'give and take' situation and both sides have their regrets.

The next day found Beth a little less critical of her Argument. As the wait for a verdict continued, Beth had to reflect on the most popular movie of 2006 which was ***Mission Impossible III.*** Trying the Boris Graham case certainly could be considered an impossible mission since it was seven years old and Beth had to rely on some of the most unsavory characters she ever had to call as prosecution witnesses.

Beth had to think maybe there is something about taking on impossible missions like this Boris Graham trial. She didn't want to admit to herself that she thrived on taking on such challenging cases. Her whole persona is that she can do the impossible. She seems to take an inner satisfaction when she is able to pull off the unbelievable verdicts.

Fortunately, in this Graham case, Beth didn't have to wait too long. In only a day and a half the jury was able to reach their verdict of guilty on every count and found all the special allegations to be true. Several weeks later the defendant, Boris Graham, was back to court. At that time the judge sentenced the defendant to Life in prison without the possibility of parole.

Beth seldom gives interviews to the news media. However, after Boris was sentenced, she was willing to talk to the press and said, "This has been an eight-year-long struggle for the Rawlings family. This is a tremendous relief knowing that the guy who terrorized their family is going away for the rest of his life."

Beth has remained to be one of the lead prosecutors in the Major Crime Division and has continued to try the toughest homicide cases. When the DA's Office was faced with the biggest serial killer trial, it was only natural that gigantic case was assigned to Beth. She did an extraordinary job on the Lonnie Franklin Jr. case better known as the 'Grim Sleeper' murders. She convicted him of murdering 10 women in South Los Angeles. This was a huge case that covered rape-murders that spanned 24 years.

Beth is a woman for all seasons. The Boris Graham case was what is called a 'Hand-Off' case in which the prosecutor assigned the case at the last minute is unable to try the case. Regrettably, the attorney who receives the 'hand-off' case doesn't have much time to prepare and has to assimilate a large amount of facts in a short period of time. However, in the Graham case, Beth was able to handle it and did an amazing job. Her endless self-confidence in her abilities pays off in arduous situations like this one. When she was given this case to try, she didn't waste time complaining about receiving a hand-off but concentrated on what needed to be done.

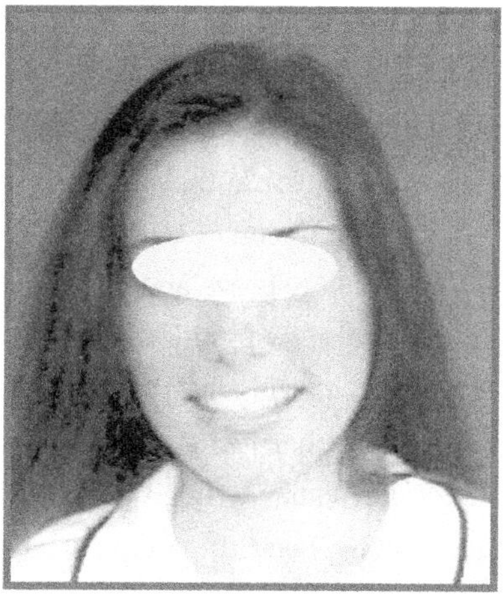

LORIE RAWLINGS

Many people would consider Lorie a super-hero. How smart it was for her not to confront the robbers in the garage. Next she had the good sense to pick up her phone in the kitchen to call the police. Then she grabbed her children to find a place where they would be safe from the robbers. Some people might criticize her actions by claiming that she didn't use good judgment by hiding her children on a narrow ledge on the roof of their two-story house.

There are those who would say that she should have initially taken her older daughter and they both should have run out the front door. In all likelihood the robbers would not have harmed her infant who was alone upstairs in a crib. Of course, there isn't any way to know for certain how the robbers would have reacted upon seeing an infant playing in a crib.

Other people might criticize Lorie by saying that she should have hid with her children in an upstairs closet or locked themselves in a bathroom. Even others like to place a 'guilt trip' on Lorie for calling the police. They say that if the police hadn't been called the robbers would have taken whatever valuables they were able to find and happily leave the house. In this scenario Christopher would be alive albeit minus a Bentley and his Rolex watch all of which the insurance company would have replaced.

Some even blamed Christopher for what happened to him. If Christopher hadn't exhibited his fancy car and being decked out with a Rolex watch and flashy jewelry, the robbers wouldn't have noticed him. Some say that if you flaunt it you lose it. Maybe it shouldn't be that way, however when living in an urban environment one has to make concessions in order to survive.

After 43 years as a prosecutor I, the author, have seen so many tragic situations where a victim has to make a split-second decision and live with the consequences. To me, Lorie Rawlings was incredibly brave and wise to quickly assess the situation and develop a game plan to protect her family from harm. The idea of hiding on the ledge was daring but the proof of the situation was that she executed this plan flawlessly and her children weren't harmed.

I don't know if the city of Woodland Hills has a 'Mother of the Year' award. If there was one, Lorie should have been the recipient of such an award. Her quick thinking and heroic actions should be lauded by all. There are always cynics who want to second-guess what victims do. However, if they were faced with a similar situation it is unlikely, they would have demonstrated such courage and bravery.

CHRISTOPHER RAWLINGS

Not everything is what it seems. This is true about Christopher who was a businessman and part owner of the Gentleman's Quarters men's clothing store in Encino. However, there was another side of Christopher Rawlings story that this book didn't dwell on. There were many elderly individuals who claimed that one of

Christopher's phone bank companies defrauded them out of their life savings. This book didn't want to be side tracked by Christopher's other activities.

For those who want the complete story about Christopher Rawlings you may want to run his name on the internet. Afterward reading about him, you may change your mind as to who are the Good Guys and who are the Bad Guys. There are many elderly folks who claim that they were defrauded by Christopher's company. We know that Kirell and Boris were bad guys who wanted to steal items from the very RICH while Christopher's alleged boiler room defrauded thousands of dollars from the POOR. The $64,000 question is who is the 'evilest dude' Kirell, Boris or Christopher?

If Christopher had lived, he might have been indicated and if convicted he could have served several years in a minimum federal prison. However, Kirell and Boris on the other hand will be serving the rest of their lives in state prison for a residential robbery which resulted in a person's death. How does that seem FAIR? The answer may be that FAIR and JUST are merely words found in the dictionary and seldom found in reality.

BORIS GRAHAM

At the time of sentencing Boris was 37 years old and had spent his entire life in or around the Pacoima area. He was a member of the local Piru Pacoima Bloods gang.

As a juvenile he was in and out of Juvenile Hall and as an adult he rotated in and out of the criminal justice system. Some people might sum up his life as a 'born loser.' Yet he was smart enough to evade the police for almost five years.

KIRELL TAYLOR

Kirell likewise grew up in Pacoima and was a member of the Piru Pacoima Bloods. He lived with his grandmother who had a staff job with the Sheriff's Department in the Jail Division. Kirell had girlfriends who helped him out when he needed it. One of his girlfriends was willing to drive him to places where he and his crime partner would commit residential robberies.

It is hard to know what motivated him to rob innocent people he didn't even know. He most likely felt that it was unfair for some to have so much while he had to struggle for the little he could get. The taking from the rich to give to the poor was merely the enforcement of the old Robin Hood theory. (Unfortunately, the real Robin Hood of Nottingham character may not have been as honorable as storytellers depict him. Robin had great distain for the noblemen and clergy and didn't mind taking from them. It's true that Robin and his jolly men did rob from the rich to give to the poor. However, the evidence isn't all that clear that he gave all that much to the poor. Basically, Robin was less than honorable and could better be described more as an opportunist than a mere common thief.)

Kirell's justification for his residential robberies seemed fair to him he just took from the affluent residents who had plenty. Anything he took would be totally replaced by everyone's homeowner's insurance. In some situations, the victim would receive a brand-new replacement for the thing stolen. He looked at his residential robberies as a condition where everyone came out a winner (except the insurance company).

Kirell was no dummy. As illustrated in his cross-examination of the DNA expert, Kirell had the smarts to be able to be successful. He demonstrated that he had the capacity to grasp the scientific basis for DNA. Although Kirell might not have been the most effective attorney in his case, he showed an aptitude for handling difficult situations with a confident flair. He believed that if he was given a chance, he would have been accepted into the US Army and would have succeeded as a soldier. Yet, some might question whether his hostile attitude against authority figures might have stifled his military career.

CHAPTER 38- WHAT HAVE WE LEARNED?

SENTENCING DILEMMA

For many years, the American Criminal Justice System has decided to take misfits like Kirell and Boris and dump them in prisons and throw away the keys. Both Kirell and Boris were sentenced to Life without the possibility of parole better known in the legal circles as LWOP. Such lengthy sentences, certainly means that the public will not be victimized by either of them as long as they are locked up.

Since Kirell was only 25 at the time of sentencing, he easily could spend another 50 years behind bars. The state of California estimates that the average cost of incarcerating an inmate in prison is about $71,000 a year. (A large part of the cost is due to security and inmate health care especially as they get older) There are those who will be able to do the math in their head while others will grab a calculator to figure out how much Kirell will cost us as taxpayers over 50 years the total being ($3,550,000). If the question is whether Kirell's life is worth that amount, many would shake their heads.

State legislators have found it popular to make more crimes eligible for Life without the Possibility of Parole. The result is that now the state prisons in California have thousands of so-called LWOP prisoners. At the same time, the voters have enacted the **Three Strikes Law.** This increased many criminal defendants' prison sentences. A defendant who has two felony convictions, upon being convicted of a third felony, which is classified as a serious crime, will be sentenced to 25 years in prison.

Some may say that locking up criminals (Bad Dudes) and placing them in prisons has not stopped crime. They are right in that there are still crimes committed by others. However, the frequency of the number of crimes has statistically been reduced and the streets are safer for everyone. There are those in the media who don't want to admit that incarceration of ne'er-do-wells reduces crime in the communities. For years the media wanted to claim that the crime rate was tied to the condition of the economy. Their theory was that people commit more crime the more dire the economy becomes. Yet when the economy tanked as in 2008 (the almost Depression) the crime rate didn't automatically increase just because people were unemployed and had less income.

The idea that crime is directly tied to how well the economy does is a mere misconception. In reality, the 'lock them up and throw away the key' philosophy has made the public far safer. However, the real issue is AT WHAT COSTS?

In order for the state legislators and state leadership to appear to be doing something, they decided to stop building additional prisons to house all the new inmates. As a result, the California prisons were overflowing with prisoners. In order to handle the influx of prisoners, the prisons started to use any available space. The prisons started converting gymnasiums and meeting halls into prison bunk housing. It wasn't long before prisoners began to file lawsuits in the federal courts regarding the overcrowded conditions in the prisons. What followed was that the federal courts ordered immediate reduction of the number of persons incarcerated in the prisons.

The bottom line was that federal judges were making the decisions as to how many prisoners could be housed at an institution. The state leaders reacted by passing legislation which transferred many state prisoners to the county jails. Since the county jails were over-crowded, the local Sheriffs developed early-release programs in order to stay below their maximum capacity limits. With all this early release activity, many bad dudes were returned to society where they have taken up their old ways of robbing and stealing from the public.

Now with this new dilemma what should happen to criminals like Kirell? Most readers would agree that Kirell should spend a certain amount of time behind bars. Hypothetically, could a person like Kirell be released after serving possibly 10 or 20 years in prison? Since he had been sentenced to Life without possibility of parole, he wasn't eligible for early release. However, if the law were changed would he be a good candidate for parole? Remember earlier, he had been given a chance to reform himself when he was given the chance of parole for robbery when he committed the Rawlings crimes. Apparently, the parole system didn't instill in Kirell a desire to change his ways of robbing innocent people.

If Kirell were released on parole again, he would require a 24 /7 parole agent to closely monitor all of his activities. It is doubtful that the government would be willing to spend the funds necessary to sufficiently monitor a person like Kirell. There are certain people like Kirell that don't lend themselves to early releases on parole.

BLACKS ARE TREATED UNFAIRLY

Some groups believe that many of the young black males are innocent of crimes they are charged with. They claim that the police target these black youths as part of the so-called 'Usual Suspects' campaign. Since Kirell is **BLACK**, some might suppose that the police must have targeted him and somehow fabricated the charges that he was involved in a residential robbery.

This idea of targeting minorities is often perpetuated by certain groups especially by relatives of **BLACK** defendants. As a matter of fact, Kirell Taylor's mother was very vocal with the news media claiming, "My son is innocent." The news media takes such comments and publicizes them. The public hears the one-sided reporting and begins to believe them. Even defendant Kirell told the newspaper reporters how innocent he was and told them as follows, "On the night of the incident I was relaxing at home with my family watching TV." This is what the public reads in the newspapers and hears on television.

The police or prosecutors can't discuss the facts of the case before the trial since they don't want to be accused of prejudicing the defendant. The mere fact that a defendant or a relative claim that the police have charged an innocent man, doesn't make it true.

However, in Kirell's case, as you the reader knows, Kirell later admitted to committing the Rawlings crime. He even explained in detail how the two of them pulled off the residential robbery. Therefore, the idea that the police framed an innocent **BLACK** doesn't fit Kirell's case.

Another group of protesters claim that **BLACK** males receive much harsher sentences because they are charged with certain narcotics charges. This claim is based on the fact that Possession and sale of Crack (It is a free base form of cocaine that can be smoked and results in short but intense high for the smoker) was made a crime with very lengthy sentences in prison. The harsh sentences were thought to be a good thing since many politicians wanted to try to eradicate Crack epidemic since it was so devastating in the Black community.

However, it was later determined that many of the sellers of Crack turned out to be Black. Then certain groups claimed that the sentencing laws on Crack were more severe than the sentencing on Cocaine offenses. The argument was that Whites are more likely to be charged with Cocaine violations while Black are more likely to be charged with Crack. Therefore, the Blacks end up with longer sentences in prison for narcotic violations.

Fortunately, this disparity of sentencing over the type of narcotic involved doesn't apply to either of our defendants since no narcotic charges were involved

Also, the **Three Strikes Law** is often blamed for the lengthy sentences **BLACK** males receive. Many states were tired of the revolving door policy in that criminals were arrested; prosecuted; convicted; sentenced to prison and within a couple of years they were back in the community committing crime. With this frustration the public decided to act and passed laws stating if a defendant had two prior felony convictions and if he or she was convicted of a third one the sentence would be 25 years to life.

It didn't take long before the prisons were inundated with 'Three Strikers' and had to house them for a long time. Since many defendants who commit crime were Black, a disproportionate of the prison population was Black. As the infamous TV star of Baretta, Robert Blake, often said, "If you can't do the time , don't do the crime."

Although the Three Strikes law did apply to both Kirell and Boris, it didn't affect their sentence. Both these defendants received Life Without Possibility of Parole before receiving any additional time from the Three Strikes sentencing law. One can argue the merits or short comings of the Three Strikes law, it didn't have any impact in either Kirell or Boris' lengthy prison sentences.

Others may claim that **BLACK** defendants don't have the opportunity to have high-priced private Defense attorneys to assist them in court. The example that is commonly given is that OJ Simpson had the money to hire the 'Dream Team' of attorneys and as a result those attorneys were able to win a not-guilty verdict for him (this is whether you believe him to be guilty or not). Nonetheless, the argument is that Blacks are at a disadvantage because they don't have the services of private attorneys to get them off the charges or obtain a reduced sentence.

To some groups this argument may seem to make sense, however the real facts don't add up. Years ago, appellate courts required all defendants to receive free attorneys to represent them in court on criminal matters in which they might be sentenced to jail or prison.

In most states **public defenders** are appointed to represent anyone who is without funds to hire their own attorney. All defendants are provided an attorney to assist them with their criminal matters. However, some people claim that **public attorneys** aren't as good as private attorneys.

This is a debate that has gone on for years. From my years of experience in courtrooms, I, the author, have found that **public defenders** are more knowledgeable of judges and court proceeding than most of the private attorneys. Often private attorneys are less familiar with the judges and the common practices of the courts while the public defenders are in court every day. In other words, the argument that **BLACKS** don't have the advantage of being represented by expensive private attorneys, may be a hollow argument since the facts don't seem to support it.

The general criticism of the American Criminal Justice System doesn't seem to apply to Kirell and Boris. They weren't innocent individuals who were unfairly targeted by the police and prosecutors.. A more compelling argument can be made that both Kirell and Boris had a poor childhood which caused them to make bad choices later in their life. The schools may have failed them and definitely their families have failed them. As youths growing up in the Pacoima area, their role models were drug dealers or hardcore gangbangers. Some can argue that it is society that is responsible for so many **BLACK** young men ending up incarcerated for the rest of their lives.

CHAPTER 39- WHAT WE NEED TO DO

MEDIA & GROUP ATTACKS ON LAW ENFORCEMENT

Back to the original question which was what should happen to Kirell and Boris? Should they be locked up for the rest of their lives or not? You can debate that question forever. However, what I want to address in this book is the larger question. Should certain groups and the news media continually criticize law enforcement for being racially motivated against BLACKS? Without a doubt this is a highly emotionally charged issue.

Most people and the media don't want to claim that the police are always the bad guys. However, the public perception often seems that way. The world has entered the digital age with its so-called Social Media phenomenal. Practically every person has a cell phone which comes with a built-in camera and recording device. The result is that any person can instantly record whatever is happening around him or her. Nowadays whenever a police officer comes in contact with a person there is a strong likelihood that someone will be video recording every move and statement the officer makes.

This new climate of scrutinizing ever action of a police officer has made the officers think they are working in 'fish bowl.' Anything the officer says and does can be placed on social media for the world to see and hear. Many groups believe that such transparency helps the community to police the police. That can be true if the entire situation has been recorded but in most situations the recording is started part way through a confrontation. Often the recording doesn't show what lead up to the confrontation, thereby giving an incomplete picture of what happened.

Putting aside the fact that the recording isn't complete there is the issue of inciting a confrontation. Often the officer makes a request to which the other party refuses to cooperate. This becomes a confrontational situation which requires the officer to use certain force to get the person to cooperate. This is where it often looks bad for the officer when he tries to arrest or handcuff a noncooperative individual.

Years ago, no one resisted the commands of a law enforcement officer. Back in Dick Tracy's day when the officer said, "Stop or I will shoot." The individual didn't weigh his alternatives such as a civil lawsuit against the officer. In the old days the robber or crook raised his hands and stopped running. The reason why he immediately complied was he didn't want to be shot by the officer. I, the author, remember a situation in which the officer shot at an escaping felon. The police report alluded to the fact that the officer had to shot at the escapee in order to protect society from this felon.

However, after years of lawsuits, the courts have placed more restrictions on police using deadly force. Nowadays a criminal who is injured in an officer shooting more than likely will have his family financially taken care for life. One may wonder what caused this turn of events. The answer is that attorneys are able to convince jurors to impose giant settlements for suspect's families.

For many years law enforcement was revered by the public and seldom was there any criticism of the police officers or police departments. However, times have changed and no longer are law enforcement officials looked upon with high respect. The trust and faith that society had once placed in their law enforcement was attributable to several reasons.

First, society wanted to support those who were hired to protect their safety from lawbreakers such as thieves, burglars or robbers. The more supportive the public was of the police the safer the community felt.

The second reason was that police officers are required to make split-second decisions often when the officer doesn't have all the facts. The public recognized that some of those split-second decisions may be in error but those mistakes do happen. The public didn't believe that the police had sinister motives when mistakes were made.

However, over time the news media and certain groups have become much more willing to criticize the police. What has caught the attention of so many are the video clips showing officer using what appears to be Excessive Force. The infamous Rodney King (who was Black) video tape showed four LAPD police officers using their batons on Mr. King when he was on the ground. Mr. King may have resisted the commends of the officers, but it was the continual beating by the officers after Mr. King stopped resisting that became the issue. The media continued to play the video tape over and over to the point that it was indelibly seared into their minds.

The result was that the officers were prosecuted for their action of using Excessive Force. When a Simi Valley jury acquitted the officers, the result was the Los Angeles Race Riot of 1992 in which 63 individuals were killed and 2,383 were injured. The property damage was over a billion dollars and resulted in more than 12,000 arrests. Many felt a justification for the riot was of the Excessive Force the officers used and got away with.

In the **BLACK** community there has been great concern that Black males were unfairly treated. Now groups who distrust the police will seize upon a short video clip showing Excessive Force as support for their political agenda that police are racially motivated. The impacted on the Black community is that they believe they have a right to resist since this is their method of civil disobedience.

These days officers are taught to **DE-ESCALATE SITUATIONS** where certain people want to be disruptive.

Without a doubt the issue of **EXCESSIVE FORCE** by the police is an issue that must be addressed by all concerned. That debate is heated but necessary. However, what the news media and certain groups may not realize is that their attack on the law enforcement is so broad that many police officers and detectives feel the wrath being directed to everyone in law enforcement. Most in the media would want law enforcement to do their job of keeping the peace in the community.

One of the purposes of writing this book is to expose the public and you the reader to how delicate a balance there is between motivating police detectives to diligently investigate their cases and criticizing the officers who may appear to be heavy-handed.

The media and certain groups attack the entire police department by claiming that they are all racist in the way they approach and handle **BLACKS** in their jurisdiction. This argument of blaming everyone who works for the police department causes morale problems. No one wants the detectives to be less vigorous in conducting a thorough investigation of any and all crimes committed within their jurisdiction.

The emphasis within the Criminal Justice System is constantly changing. There are times the public wants to lock up the bad dudes for as long as possible. Other times the emphasis is on rehabilitation and being more understanding of the frailties of the less fortunate. The public wants safe streets and often they blame the police for the increase of crime. The fickle public may claim that if the police were more aggressive in doing their job there wouldn't be as much crime.

The barrage of Negative Criticism of the police has a price. If the public wants to criticize the police for everything they do, the result is that police won't do anything. They will avoid conflict and eventually a mild form of anarchy will set in. If the public want criminals to be caught, then they need to encourage the officers and detectives to thoroughly investigate criminal matters.

Unfortunately, few people realize all the steps detectives go through when investigating any type of crime especially a homicide. Most of the clues go nowhere. An experienced detective gains a sense of knowing which clues are worth investigating and which ones are best put on the back burner. Clues come in various forms and situations. The easy ones which are very tempting to pursue. And there are clues that consume so much time and resources that the detective has to question whether they are worth pursuing.

This case involving Boris and Kirell an informant provided specific material that sounded great but turned out to be bogus. This is where a detective could fall into easy traps and as a result the case may self-destruct. The outstanding homicide detectives are best described as being: **Tenacious, Stubborn, Persistent, Dogged, Steadfast** and many more similar words that can be found in any thesaurus.

A good homicide detective has to be resilient. They develop thick skin to allow them to handle one disappointment after another. They have to stay focused when everything is crumbling around them. They have to be knowledgeable of human nature and be willing to go down risky roads not knowing where they will lead.

Just to illustrate in some of the ways the police are criticized would be to look at the Rawlings case. On the night of the car crash the officers responded to a traffic accident between the Bentley and the small Chevrolet. As a result of that accident, hundreds of legal documents that were in the Chevrolet went flying all over the street.

The driver of the Chevrolet was an attorney who was working on a civil matter involving thousands of legal documents. When his Chevrolet was totally demolished many of his legal documents went flying all over the roadway. Since the attorney was injured, he was transported to the hospital and he wasn't able to retrieve all his papers.

It was raining on the night of the crash and there were live high voltage lines arcing, the officers were more concerned with the accident scene and finding the suspects. In other words, no officer went around collecting the soggy legal documents. The below photos show what a mess had been created as a result of the accident which was not the fault of the police.

The attorney complained to LAPD for not assigning officers to retrieve the legal documents. The point is that it is easy to blame the police for something they had no control over. The head detective did feel bad about the situation in that the legal documents weren't ever retrieved. Whose responsibility was it to pick up the soggy documents? Should the tow truck driver have done it? Should the public works personnel clean up the litter? Bottom line is that everyone wants to blame the police department for whatever happens, even if it isn't part of their job description.

Those who make blanket criticism of the police may not understand the harm they are doing. At some point the detectives of the world will lose their willingness to go out of their way to solve their cases. It is easier and less controversial to merely investigate a crime while sitting behind a desk in a police station.

However, we need persistent detectives who are willing to go into the field and investigate clues and pursue all leads in a case. The actions of the civilian witness Colliers and the detectives were a pivotal part of this case. Thank God for the detectives' tenaciousness to do things they didn't have to do.

Homicide detectives tend to be skeptical people because of all the unbelievable rejections they face during an investigation. They have to be motivated to go that extra mile. Few individuals are able to withstand all the disappointments homicide detectives endure. That may be the reason that veteran homicide detectives seem to be slightly grumpy people with a negative attitude. To them the glass is half empty.

Just look at this Rawlings case with all the clues that turned out to be worthless. A less motivated detective could easily have given up. Small and large police departments want to motivate their detectives to be steadfast and willing to take the extra step to solve the crime. Hopefully the constant harassing from the media and vocal groups will not turn off those dogged detectives. They are merely trying to do their jobs in a hostile anti-law enforcement environment.

We as a society have to be aware that on the other side of the thin blue line lurks anarchy and injustice. Let's learn from this book that good detective work needs to be encouraged and recognized wherever it exists.

Sherlock Holmes is a fictitious detective who wasn't working on real homicide cases. He is better known for his brilliant way of unraveling facts to catch the elusive killers. Holmes was quoted as saying "It is a capital mistake to theorize in advance of the facts. Insensibly one begins to twist facts to suit theories instead of theories to suit the facts." With all that arduous work that the LAPD homicide detectives went through to apprehend these two culprits, Kirell Taylor and Boris Graham, Sherlock Holmes likely said, "TENACITY SOLVED THE MURDER!"

Made in the USA
Monee, IL
04 November 2026

67386556R00134